D0642777

Aid Climbing with Mike Corbett

Aid Climbing with Mike Corbett

Mike Corbett and Steve Boga

STACKPOLE
BOOKS

Published by
STACKPOLE BOOKS
5067 Ritter Road
Mechanicsburg, PA 17055

Printed in the United States of America

10 9 8 7 6 5 4 3 2 1

First edition

Cover photo by Chris Falkenstein: Mike Corbett belays on the ledge below as Rich Albuschkat leads the final pitch of the Lost Arrow Spire, Yosemite National Park.

Cover design by Mark Olszewski

Library of Congress Cataloging-in-Publication Data

Corbett, Mike, 1953–
    Aid climbing with Mike Corbett / Mike Corbett and Steven Boga. — 1st ed.
        p.   cm.
    ISBN 0-8117-2417-4
    1. Rock climbing. 2. Rock climbing—Equipment and supplies.
I. Boga, Steve, 1947–   . II. Title.
GV200.2.C66   1995
796.5'223—dc20   94-47517
                                                                      CIP

Contents

An Important Note to Readers

This book contains much useful information about the sport of rock climbing. Before engaging in this potentially hazardous sport, however, you must do more than read a book.

The sport requires skill, concentration, physical strength and endurance, proper equipment, knowledge of fundamental principles and techniques, and unwavering commitment to your own safety and that of your companions.

The publisher and authors obviously cannot be responsible for your safety. Because rock climbing entails the risk of serious and even fatal injury, we emphasize that you should not begin climbing except under expert supervision. No book can substitute for proper training and experience under the guidance and supervision of a qualified teacher.

Introduction

If a blade of grass can grow out of a crack, then a piton should be able to fit in that crack.

—JOHN SALATHE

John Salathe, the father of big-wall climbing, was talking about sixth-class, or aid, climbing, which happens to be my specialty. When the rock is too steep or too smooth for climbers to rely solely on the natural holds offered by the rock, we use aids, artificially creating our own footholds and handholds with etriers, little ladders made of nylon webbing.

When I began the outdoor life at sixteen as a backpacker, my biggest challenge was keeping the bears away from my food. A group of my backpacking friends were climbers. "Try it once," they said. Initially, I didn't think climbing had much to offer. I felt intimidated by it, didn't see myself as a climber.

Then one day, I snapped under the pressure. "Okay, I'll try it once. If I don't like it, will you leave me alone?!"

"Oh, yes," they promised.

I tried it and, of course, I loved it. I was immediately hooked. I went climbing the next day, and the next, and the next . . . I loved the exercise, the excitement. It was thrilling. And I was learning something new. I didn't realize it at the time, but I needed something new.

My friend Richard let me lead. Within a couple of weeks, I was leading 5.7 pitches, using only chocks. I was learning so much, I thought my head would explode. I was so excited that I would stay up late practicing knots, tying them over and over, doing them with my eyes closed.

I learned the climbing classifications:

Class 1: Walking

Class 2: Hiking—boots recommended

Class 3: Scrambling—handholds and footholds, ropes not required

Class 4: Free climbing—using rope with belays, and lots of big handholds and footholds

Class 5: Free climbing—using rope with belays and protection, rated 5.0 to 5.14

Class 6: Direct aid—artificial handholds and footholds created by your equipment

I bought books, such as *Basic Rockcraft* by Royal Robbins and *Ropes, Knots and Slings* by Walt Wheelock, and began reading everything I could about climbing. I became totally absorbed in this unusual new sport. It was the start of a fever that's lasted twenty years.

Less than a year after my first climb, as I looked up at the vertiginous granite walls of Yosemite, I realized that the only way I could scale them was by learning to aid-climb. I decided to do some research.

I began watching aid climbers, asking questions. What do I need to aid-climb? Where can I practice? I learned that all the big Yosemite climbs, even if they were free-climbed subsequently, were originally done with aid-climbing techniques; that Yosemite is possibly the single most important area for aid climbing; that much of the state-of-the-art equipment was developed in Yosemite; that people came from all over the world to improve their aid-climbing techniques.

Eventually I found partners who had similar interests. As in free climbing, I started at the bottom, in this case A1, the easiest aid climbing available. If I fell, I would drop no more than one placement, less than 10 feet. Step by step, I learned the techniques and strategies that enabled me to reach higher levels.

As I became more efficient, I began doing harder routes. After doing several overnight climbs, I turned my attention to the mother of all aid climbs: El Capitan. I quickly learned that a climber has to be efficient to make it up El Capitan. It's one thing to follow someone else but quite another to lead such a climb. Leading capably required so much more—like experience. Today I have that experience, having led all or part of fifty El Capitan climbs.

Aid climbing has been called rock engineering. Admittedly, it's not as graceful as free climbing. But aid will take you places you never dreamed of going free, and it's tremendously satisfying getting up sixth-class rock and doing it right.

– 1 –

History of Aid Climbing

Some climbing historians date the origin of aid climbing to June 1492, when France's Charles VIII ordered his chamberlain, Antoine de Ville, and a handful of companions to scale Mont Aiguille (6,783 feet). To reach the summit of what was previously believed to be an unassailable peak, the de Ville party used aid in the form of wooden ladders.

Most climbers, however, view the 1786 ascent of Mont Blanc, which also required wooden ladders, as the true beginning of aid climbing. In the eighteenth and nineteenth centuries, it was not uncommon for guides and porters to lug heavy wooden ladders to the base of difficult rock steps.

Artificial aids were scorned by many climbers, and as alpine clubs were organized, opposition grew to what mountaineer Geoffrey Winthrop Young termed "publicity stunting and mechanical acrobatics."

Despite such vocal opposition, history is replete with accounts of artificial climbing on many important first ascents prior to the twentieth century. In Yosemite, aid was used by Scotsman George Anderson to ascend the "inaccessible" Half Dome in 1875. In an engineering feat that took six weeks, he drilled bolts in the granite dome and strung a rope ladder to the summit. The oft-photographed Devil's Tower in Wyoming received its first ascent in 1893 via a 350-foot wooden ladder hammered into cracks.

Aid climbing really started to take hold after the turn of the twen-

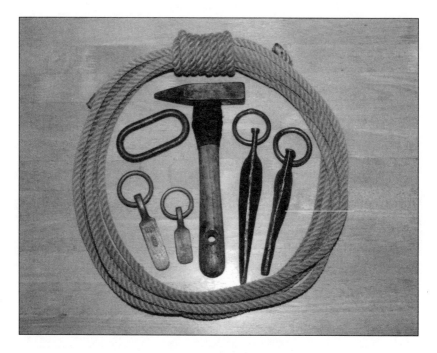

Equipment from the World War II era: A gold line rope surrounds (*clockwise from top left*) a steel carabiner, an Austrian piton hammer, two soft metal ring angle pitons, and two soft metal ring wafer pitons.

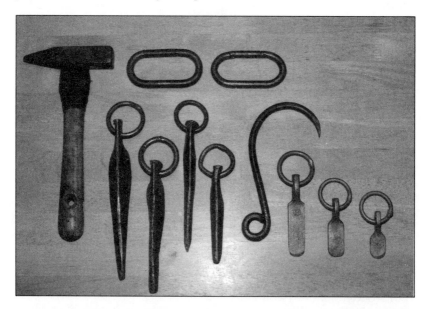

None of this equipment from the 1940s would be used by today's climbers. *Top:* two steel carabiners. *From left:* a lightweight piton hammer, four ring angle pitons, a sky hook, and three ring wafer pitons.

tieth century, spurred by improvements in equipment, especially pitons and carabiners. Used in conjunction with the climbing rope, better equipment permitted better technique. Europeans, who had been responsible for most of these advances, could now attack steeper, more difficult faces. Some of the great spires of the European Alps were climbed, though not without a price. The death toll soared as climbers tried to push their equipment beyond its limits.

It would take a Swiss-born blacksmith named John Salathé to upgrade the equipment for the next climbing breakthrough. Salathé moved to California and began a climbing career at age forty-six. He discovered that the soft iron pitons imported from Europe were no match for the hard granite cliffs of Yosemite. One day he was climbing a crack that narrowed to almost nothing. Upon closer investigation, he saw a blade of grass growing out of the minute crack. "If a blade of grass can come out," he thought, "a piton can go in." But when he tried to drive in an iron piton, it just bent.

Using his knowledge as a metal worker, Salathé hand-forged a piton from strips of high-strength carbon steel salvaged from discarded Model A axles, creating the first hard steel pitons in the world. Then he returned to the tiny crack. As he later told the story in his heavy Swiss accent, "I took my piton and I pound and pound, and it goes into the rock." Salathé, whom Yvon Chouinard would call "the father of big-wall climbing," was now able to nail up hitherto hopeless cracks and thus avoid the need for bolts. Even today, fifty years later, Salathé's Lost Arrow design is regarded as the best for small pitons.

The effect was to revolutionize both free climbing and aid climbing. Freed of the burden of lugging extra backup pitons to replace ruined ones, climbers were able to carry more food and water, allowing them to attempt longer and more arduous faces. The twelve years after the introduction of Salathé's pitons saw every major cliff in Yosemite climbed: Lost Arrow Spire in 1946; Sentinel Rock in 1950; the great Northwest Face of Half Dome in 1957; El Capitan in 1958. It was the realization of what climber-photographer Galen Rowell would call "Yosemite's potential as the ideal locale for testing human limits on rock."

In the early fifties, California climber Chuck Wilts invented the knife-blade piton, using chrome-molybdenum aircraft steel for the first time. These pitons, smaller than anything available at the time, could fit in cracks no wider than a dime.

Although most of Europe's major rock faces had been ascended by the time climbing caught on in the United States, Americans now took the lead in aid climbing, especially on big walls. In 1957, when Royal Robbins, Jerry Gallwas, and Mike Sherrick climbed the Northwest Face of Half Dome, it catapulted Yosemite to the forefront of big-wall aid climbing, a position it would hold for several decades.

In 1958, in a monumental engineering feat that received a lot of attention, Warren Harding and various partners conquered the South Buttress of El Capitan, the most difficult and technical aid climb in the world. Three years later, Royal Robbins, regarded as the finest aid climber in the world, teamed up with Chuck Pratt and Tom Frost to climb the Salathé Wall on El Capitan, named for their innovative predecessor.

Many climbers today still regard the Salathé Wall as the finest rock climb in the world. And although it has been climbed without aid, most climbers still employ aid moves to scale this classic route.

Royal Robbins and his peers were far from done. In 1964, Robbins, Yvon Chouinard, Frost, and Pratt completed the extremely strenuous North America Wall on El Capitan, which was immediately given the title "most difficult aid climb in the world." It seemed that each time Yosemite climbers found a new climb, it acquired that reputation.

Yvon Chouinard, like John Salathé, had a huge impact on both equipment design and ethical standards. His invention of the rurp (realized ultimate reality piton), a tiny postage-stamp-sized piton that could fit in a crack no wider than a blade of grass, helped to reduce the need for placing bolts. Chouinard also designed the chock, a piece of hardware that fits securely in a crack or behind a flake, greatly reducing the damage that results from repeated piton placements. In fact, it was Chouinard who spearheaded the movement toward clean climbing that took hold in the seventies.

If Royal Robbins was the most prolific aid climber of the sixties, Jim Bridwell was the dominant force of the seventies and eighties. His ascents of aid routes with names like "Sea of Dreams," "The Big Chill," and "Zenyatta Mondatta" are among the most difficult aid climbs in existence. Perhaps the zenith of aid climbing was Bridwell and team's 1978 ascent of the "Pacific Ocean Wall" on El Capitan. A climb that demanded several tricky aid placements—mainly rurps, copperheads, and hooks—it set the standard for today's strenuous aid climbs.

Also in 1978, free climber Ray Jardine began marketing the Friend, a spring-loaded camming device that gripped a crack to provide a bombproof anchor. Friends and other camming devices have promoted clean climbing and permitted safer climbing of loose, dicey rock.

Today's aid climbers use a variety of protective devices, including cams, chocks, hooks, copperheads, and yes, pitons. Despite significant advances in the quality of climbing equipment, the sport's risk hasn't been totally eliminated. Aid climbers routinely risk falls of a hundred feet or more in their quest for height.

What does the future hold for aid climbing? Clean climbing—that is, without pitons—will continue to grow in step with environmental awareness. As equipment continues to improve, some longer aid climbs will cease to be multiday events, and fewer bivouacs will be needed. And perhaps someone will invent a new gizmo that will replace the destructive but heretofore necessary piton.

Just as long as they don't come up with something that eliminates the actual climbing.

– 2 –

Equipment

Ropes

Modern ropes have come a long way from the horsehair ones used in ancient Carthage or even from the hemp lines used by pre–World War II pioneers in the Alps, where snapped ropes prematurely ended the lives of many climbers. After hemp, climbing ropes were made out of flax, then cotton, followed by manila from the leafstalk of a Philippine tree and sisal from a plant in Yucatán.

During World War II, the U.S. Bureau of Standards concluded that for strength, elasticity, and durability, nylon was superior to all natural fibers. Since 1945, climbing ropes have been fashioned from nylon or Perlon, a trade name for a plastic similar to nylon.

Climbing ropes today are universally kernmantle, German for "jacketed core." Kernmantle ropes have a woven nylon sheath over braided continuous fibers of nylon.

Aid climbers use at least two ropes: one for leading, another for hauling up supplies. The standard-size rope for leading a pitch, in both aid climbing and free climbing, is 11 millimeters in diameter. The second rope is usually 8 or 9 millimeters. The standard length of climbing ropes, once 150 feet, is now 165 feet, or 50 meters.

Free climbers generally use a supple rope, something flexible that feeds out easily. But aid climbers want something more tightly woven, more abrasion-resistant. Aid ropes take more of a beating than free ropes. Not only does aid climbing demand that you clip your rope through countless pieces of protection, but it's also likely that members of your team will jumar up that rope. If so, it's easier to jumar up a stiffer rope.

If you're on a long overnight climb that might require a traverse, it would be wise to have a third rope. When lowering haul bags sideways, you don't want to pendulum them, lest you break your water bottles and smash your candy bars. Gently moving the bags sideways requires a third rope, usually 8 or 9 millimeters in thickness. This is done before the follower leaves the belay station to begin cleaning the aid pitch. Belaying the haul bag with a belay device allows the follower to lower the bag diagonally or move it horizontally, all the while controlling the speed and avoiding a reckless swing.

If you do carry three ropes, you might have an 11 millimeter for leading, an 11-millimeter for hauling, and a third rope that is 8 or 9 millimeters. That way, if the lead rope is damaged, you have a backup 11-millimeter as a replacement. Above all, don't lead an aid climb with an 8- or 9-millimeter rope. All the jumaring will chew up a smaller rope.

It's a good idea to mark the midpoint of your climbing ropes. That way, if the leader asks how much rope is left, you can answer, for example, "You just passed the halfway mark."

The two main types of climbing ropes are static and dynamic. Static ropes don't stretch. They are mostly used by cavers, but climbers sometimes find them useful as fixed ropes to be left in place. The standard rope that climbers use is dynamic. This rope stretches (about 6 percent), and the rope absorbs much of the energy generated by a falling climber. The ramifications of taking a bad fall on a rope that doesn't stretch are ugly. Imagine your body as a twig; now imagine it snapping in half.

Never use a static rope to lead a climb. Never. I did use a static rope as a second rope when I climbed El Capitan and Half Dome with paraplegic Mark Wellman. Upon reaching the end of a pitch, I would anchor a static rope for Mark so that he could use his mechanical ascenders on a rope that didn't stretch. That meant that every inch he pulled himself up the rope was an inch gained. That was important, because he had more than 40,000 inches to cover.

The two most popular brands of rope are Mammut and Edelrid, both Swiss manufacturers. The cost of a good rope seems to hover around a dollar a foot.

Rope Care. To prolong the life of your rope, take proper care of it. Shield the rope from direct sunlight whenever possible. Ultraviolet (UV) rays eat away at a rope with the insidiousness of termites undermining a house. Don't hang your rope in the sun; instead, store it in a dark, cool place. Transport it in a rope bag, a glorified stuff sack that has a zipper running its entire length. An inner sleeve allows the bag to expand when you unzip. This is a great way to carry a rope to a climb; it's also an efficient way to feed out a rope from a belay. It eliminates the messy business of having ropes dangling below you that can get tangled in cracks or on projections. The belayer, undistracted by rope management, is free to give the leader the attention he needs.

Keep your rope clean. Never lay a climbing rope in dirt or sand. Never step on a rope. Little dirt granules can work their way through the sheath (remember the termites?) and begin cutting fibers. Once you have approached a cliff and are preparing to do a climb, uncoil your rope atop a backpack, keeping it out of the dirt.

If you do soil your rope, you can wash it in a machine or by hand in a bathtub. Use a mild detergent like Woolite or one made specially for cleaning ropes. Work the soap into the rope. Rinse and hang in a dry, shady place. Do not put the rope in a dryer.

Keep stored ropes away from solvents like gasoline, kerosene, and battery acid.

When using the rope, watch out for sharp edges and projections. If your rope is rubbing up against a sharp edge, you must either move the rope or pad the edge. For padding, use a shirt, a belay seat, or whatever it takes. You don't ever want anyone in your party cleaning a pitch on a rope draped over a sharp edge. As a second jumars up such a rope, each bounce cuts ever so slightly through the rope.

One time on Half Dome, I was jumaring up a free rope—one that had been anchored above by the leader—when I noticed that the rope was caught on a quartz crystal of rock. Each time I jumared, I thought, "Oh my God, I'm sawing through this rope." If that had happened, I would have fallen, oh, about a thousand feet. When I reached the crystal, I saw that the rope was indeed sawn halfway through.

Inspect your rope often, especially after a fall of any significance. John Long, noted climber and author, assures us that "Though there are isolated cases of ropes being cut over sharp edges or chopped by rock fall, a modern climbing rope has never simply broken from the impact of a fall." So great is the safety cushion built into modern ropes that healthy ones have no chance to break, no matter how severe the fall. The operative word there is *healthy*.

The best way to check a rope for core damage is to pinch a tiny loop of it. If it pinches flat, you know the core is damaged and the rope should be replaced. If you can't pinch it flat—that is, there is still a hole in the loop big enough for your finger—the rope is okay. You should perform a thorough check on every inch of the 165 feet. It's time-consuming but well worth the effort. The worst piece of equipment a climber can have is a damaged rope.

Since you are hanging life and limb on your rope, it makes sense to listen to what the experts say about when to stop climbing on it. The conservative point of view suggests that you retire a rope after four years, even if it was only used by your grandmother on 5.4s, and after two years if it receives normal weekend use. And says Chris Gore, technical consultant for Beal ropes, "Any rope suffering a long fall of great severity should be retired immediately."

Boots

If you surveyed the climbers doing El Capitan in any given year, you would find them wearing dozens of different kinds of shoes. In my fifty climbs of El Capitan, I have worn just about every shoe imaginable, including Vasque Ascenders, which they don't make anymore, and Shoenards, which were glorified tennis shoes with toe caps. I've worn Hi Tech hiking boots, as well as Reebok and Adidas tennis shoes. I've even worn pliable free-climbing boots, because that's all I had.

The best aid-climbing boot I've ever had was the old Royal Robbins. It looked like an old hiking boot with a rubber rand around the toe for protection. It was very comfortable for aid climbing, and what made it comfortable was the stiff steel shank in the sole for support.

I strongly urge against using free-climbing boots for aid climbing. They are soft and malleable and lack arch support, which spells misery after a hard day of standing in aid ladders. They are also expensive, a consideration because you will probably ruin them on your first aid climb. Better to buy a pair of fairly stiff-soled hiking boots and apply Shoe Goo or a toe cap. To prolong the life of your boots, add Shoe Goo to the seams as well as the toes.

If I'm going to do a long overnight climb, I take both climbing footwear and a pair of tennis shoes for the hike down. When you get to the top of a long climb, your feet will cry out for a change of shoes.

Harness

Once upon a time, climbers tied their climbing ropes directly to their waists. But an arrested fall with a rope tied to your waist can yank your spleen up into your throat, and fortunately those days are past. Today most climbers use a sit-harness, made from wide nylon tape sewn together. Using a harness has several advantages over tying directly to the waist. First, it's a more convenient way to join rope and torso, and it provides loops for clipping on runners and other gear. And, in the event of an arrested fall, a harness distributes the impact force over a wider area of the body.

Choose a comfortable harness; you may wear it for hours, with several pounds of hardware dangling from it. Try on several before deciding which one to buy.

Take proper care of your harness. Read and follow all instructions carefully. Keep the harness away from caustic substances such as battery acid. Be sure to inspect your harness regularly for signs of damage.

Carabiners

Affectionately known as krabs or biners (pronounced "beaners"), carabiners are aluminum alloy snap links that work like giant safety pins. They allow you to attach a rope to the protection—pitons, chocks, or camming devices—that you put in the rock. They come in two basic shapes: oval and D. I favor the D shape, because it is stronger, opens more easily when weighted, and permits a smoother flow of rope.

A carabiner has a spring-loaded gate that opens inward to accept rope or runner and snaps closed when pressure is released from the gate. Standard-gate carabiners allow a climber to open the gate with one thumb, an important convenience when you're fiddling with equipment on a vertical wall. If carabiners are used properly—they are designed to be weighted lengthwise—they are exceptionally strong. The minimum breaking strength is 2,500 pounds, and some reach 5,000 pounds, but only if the carabiner is weighted along the major axis. Don't ever set up a biner so that the pull is straight out

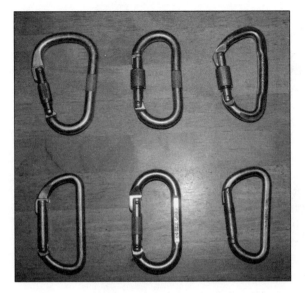

Carabiners. *Top row, left to right:* a locking D, a locking oval, and a locking ultra-light. *Bottom row, left to right:* a standard-gate D, a standard-gate oval, and a standard-gate ultra-light.

from the gate, for then the breaking strength is no greater than the gate pin—usually less than 500 pounds.

The carabiners I prefer are the heavier, beefier ones, such as Chouinard and Bonaitti; these can withstand the abuse of aid climbing. Constant grinding against hard rock and even harder pitons can create abrasive ridges that weaken carabiners. Stay away from lightweight sport-climbing biners. Even the slightly heavier free-climbing biners should be avoided. Remember that free climbing puts much less stress on biners because you don't weight them as you do in aid climbing.

I am often asked how many carabiners one should take on a climb. Let's say you're climbing the full length of a 165-foot rope. By the time you attach one end to your harness and your partner does the same, you are left with about 150 feet of usable rope. The distance between aid placements will be largely determined by your height and what the crack permits, but if the rock is steep and difficult, you might place protection every 3 feet. That means you would need fifty carabiners just to attach the rope to the aid placements. You will need additional carabiners for the belayer's anchors, for the leader's anchors after the pitch is finished, and for hauling equipment. In other words, it's not uncommon to start a pitch with seventy-five to one hundred biners.

Carabiner Care. Most carabiners are made of aircraft-quality aluminum alloy, with a life expectancy of at least ten years. Still, it is important to inspect biners periodically for disqualifying cracks. Corrosion can eat away at carabiners, leaving a fine white powder; this is especially a problem for climbers near the sea. If you have any doubts about a carabiner's viability, discard it. The expression "Better safe than sorry" has no greater applicability than in rock climbing.

If you are concerned that a carabiner might open at the wrong time, use two simultaneous carabiners, positioning them so that the gates open in opposite directions. Or use a screw-gate carabiner. Once a screw-gate is locked, it will come unlocked only when you want it to. You might be tempted to use screw-gates everywhere you use a carabiner, but it's really unnecessary. Standard-gate biners can open only if the gate strikes a projection at just the right angle. You don't normally need that extra security, and it's incredibly time-consuming to lock forty or fifty carabiners as you ascend each rope length. And, of course, your partner must unlock all of them as he or she follows to clean the pitch.

Pitons

Also called pins or pegs, pitons are chrome-molybdenum ("chrome-moly") steel spikes that are hammered into cracks to secure anchors and support climbers. Piton shapes and sizes vary, but all have an eyelet through which a carabiner or piece of webbing can be attached. Unlike other aspects of climbing technology, pitons have changed little since Yvon Chouinard began making them in the early sixties. Chouinard pitons were the best then, and they still are (though Black Diamond bought out Chouinard some years ago).

Pitons are my specialty. I know more about pitons than any other piece of equipment, because I've used so many over the years. I also have an impressive collection of old pitons in my climbing museum. But times have changed, and conscientious climbers use pitons only as a last resort, when they cannot place a chock or a spring-loaded camming device (SLCD) in a crack.

The disadvantage of pitons is that they damage the rock. Suppose I hammer a series of pitons into a crack. Because we try not to leave any pitons in the rock (it's ugly, and we may need them higher on the climb), my partner follows, removing the pitons. Future climbing parties doing the same crack will need slightly larger pitons in

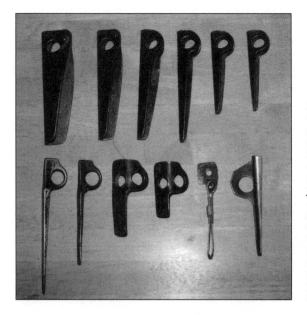

Pitons come in a variety of shapes and sizes. *Top row, from left:* 1¹/₂-inch, 1¹/₄-inch, 1-inch, ³/₄-inch, ⁵/₈-inch, and ¹/₂-inch angle pitons. *Bottom row, from left:* two Lost Arrow, or horizontal, pitons—a long thin and a medium thick; two knife-blade pitons—a medium thin and a short thin; a rurp; and a "Leeper Z" piton (similar to an angle piton).

that crack, because we've effectively chiseled out some of the rock. The crack keeps getting bigger and bigger, until what was once a nice, thin crack is now peppered with big, gaping holes called *piton scars.*

A n unexpected benefit of pitons is that they eventually enlarge a crack wide enough to permit the use of an alternate anchor, such as a camming device. When that happens, the damage stops.

Despite their disadvantages, pitons persist. They are still manufactured in this country, most successfully by Black Diamond, and climbs exist that require pitons. Pitons will continue to be used until we come up with a better method.

The smallest piton is called a *rurp* an acronym for realized ultimate reality piton. About the size of a postage stamp, it is meant to be used only for aid climbing. That is, it will hold body weight but cannot be counted on to hold a fall. A rurp is unique among pitons because it has a tiny eye—about ¼ inch in diameter—that is too small to accept a carabiner. If you have an old-style rurp, you thread a

$^9/16$-inch piece of webbing through the eye, tie a loop using a ring-bend (water) knot, then clip a carabiner to the webbing loop and attach that to the rope. Newer rurps come with a wire loop for attaching a biner. There are variations of the rurp, but all serve the same purpose of protection in small cracks.

The next largest piton is called a *knife blade*. Though knife blades come in different sizes, they are all about as thick as a butter knife. Though used primarily for aid climbing, they can be used for free climbing. Unlike rurps, knife blades are designed to hold a fall.

The next largest size is the Lost Arrow, or horizontal, piton, modeled after the original John Salathé design. Lost Arrows, usually 2 to 6 inches long, are suitable for $^1/8$- to $^3/8$-inch cracks. They will hold a fall and can be used for both free and aid climbing.

The next size, angle pitons, are pieces of metal bent into U-shaped channels to provide three points of contact with the rock: at the back and the two edges of the channel. They are big but hollow, and therefore light. They fit cracks from ½ to 1½ inches in width. The smallest angles—½-inch and $^5/8$-inch—are called *baby angles*. The ¾-inch angle is called a *standard* or *regular*. And the larger ones—1-inch, 1¼-inch, and 1½-inch—are referred to by their size. So if I'm leading and need angles, I might call down to my partner, "Hey, Joe, send me some

Aluminum bong pitons (*from left:* 2-inch, 2½-inch, 3-inch, and 4-inch) have for the most part been replaced by large camming devices, but most climbers tackling a long route still carry a few.

babies," "Send me some standards," or "Send me some inch-and-a-half angles."

A piton larger than 1½ inches is called a *bong* or *bong bong*. The name is derived from the sound it makes when hammered properly into a crack. A bong is a sheet of aluminum bent over to form a U shape, dotted with holes to make it lighter.

At one time, bongs were the only way to protect a sheer climb up a wide crack. Today bongs are still carried, but they are seldom used. They work beautifully, but climbers facing large cracks generally resort to an SLCD to minimize rock damage.

A thousand feet up El Capitan, I once had a run-in with a piton. Or rather it ran into me. I was in a party of four, with one of my partners more than two pitches above me. Suddenly I heard him yell, "Look out below! Piton!" I grabbed a daypack to use as a shield, but that piton must have had my name on it. After dropping 400 feet and reaching terminal velocity, it hit me square on the shoulder. It felt like someone had hauled off and hit me with a golf club. Next morning, I couldn't raise my arm. But I finished the climb. For weeks I had what looked like a tattoo of a Lost Arrow on my shoulder. I called it my badge of foolishness.

Chocks

Also known as *chockstones, nuts, stoppers, wedges, tapers,* or *hexentrics*, chocks are pieces of metal of various sizes and shapes, strung with cable or rope, that fit into irregularities in the rock. Imagine fitting a pebble into a crack, tying a piece of rope around that pebble, and giving it a downward tug. The stone will stop as the crack pinches or bottlenecks.

History tells us that the modern chock evolved from the British habit of tying off just such natural stones in cracks. British climbers then began using machine nuts found along the railroad tracks below climbing crags. In the sixties, manufacturers began turning out nuts specifically for rock climbing. The first such nuts were crude, but as climbers began to realize their potential, designs improved to the point that by the early seventies, they offered protection as bomb-proof as pitons.

Chocks come in two basic shapes: tapers and hexentrics. Tapers, also known as wedges or stoppers, are rectangular with sloping sides. They are perfect for flaring cracks that narrow in the back. Some tapers are offset—no parallel sides—and using them at different angles effectively produces different sizes. Be aware, though, that offsets are less reliable in marginal placements.

Tapers range from thumbnail-size micros strung with wire the diameter of dental floss to beefy 1½-inch nuts tied with Spectra cord, reputed to be stronger than steel of the same size.

Cable has replaced rope for all but the largest tapers. Not only is it stronger than rope (and usually stronger than the nut itself), but it's stiff, which allows a few extra inches of reach, often the difference between placing and not placing the protection. If a chock fails, it is almost certainly due to poor placement and not a broken cable. With extended use, however, the cable can fray beneath the head of the nut; if so, it's time to replace it.

Hexentrics, or hexes, are six-sided chocks that excel in cracks up to 3½ inches. Placed endwise, the hex is slotted in the crack like a big taper. SLCDs have largely replaced hexes in the climber's arsenal, but for a bottleneck placement, nothing beats a big hex.

Hexentrics in sizes 1 through 10 (*right to left*). Sizes 1, 2, and 3 come with a wire cable; 4 through 10 require webbing or nylon cord.

Spring-Loaded Camming Devices

The spring-loaded camming device is undoubtedly the protection most commonly used by climbers today. Developed in the seventies and marketed as the Friend by Ray Jardine in 1978, the SLCD has revolutionized climbing.

SLCDs have three or four pear-shaped lobes that are attached to an axis and controlled by a trigger. When you squeeze the trigger, it causes the device to retract, thereby becoming smaller. Keeping the trigger squeezed, a climber places the SLCD in a crack and releases the trigger, causing the cams to spring back into shape. As the SLCD expands, it grips the inside of the crack. Putting weight on that device merely causes it to tighten its grip.

Friends, easy to place, easy to remove, and bombproof, were considered cheating by some climbers of the old school. Others thought they sounded too good to be true. But they turned out to be as good as their reputation. They did no damage to the rock and opened up climbs that had previously seemed insuperable, benefits that soon

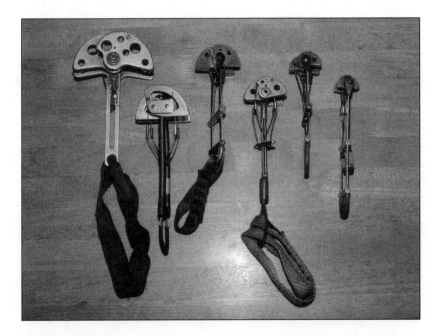

SLCDs are available from many manufacturers. *From left to right*, some of the most popular brands are the Friend, Camalot, Wired Bliss, Cassin Cam, Meto-lius T.C.U. (three-cam unit), and Hugh Banner T.C.U.

won over the skeptical. Today there is little or no vocal opposition to SLCDs.

SLCDs really show their strength in parallel-sided cracks, which are unsuitable for nuts. They are also excellent in loose rock and around expanding flakes. An expanding flake is a flake so thin that when pressure is applied, it appears to move. If you attack an expanding flake with a piton, the crack expands with the flake's movement, spits out the piton below—the one supporting you—and you fall. A camming device, on the other hand, expands to fill the crack, preventing a fall.

SLCDs come in a wide range of sizes and can fit cracks from ½ inch to 9 inches wide. Since the introduction of the Friend, there have been many SLCD copycats, as well as some significant improvements. Brand names include Camalots, Aliens, TCU (Three-Cam Units), and Wired Bliss.

If you examine a modern-day climber's arsenal, you will find it heavy on SLCDs and light on pitons. That is reflected in my own choice of protection. On my last climb of El Capitan, I carried about eight pitons, two dozen chocks, and thirty-five camming devices.

Etriers

Also called *aiders, aid slings,* and *aid ladders,* etriers are made of 1-inch flat webbing (as opposed to tubular webbing) tied to create a ladder in which climbers can stand. Etriers range from three to five rungs, and which you choose may be governed by how tall you are. In either case, they are small and lightweight.

Etriers used to be made of wooden rungs threaded onto rope. Later, aluminum replaced the wood. That made the ladder lighter, but it still didn't pack well. Etriers made of webbing, on the other hand, can be wadded up and stuffed into packs. Although it might seem easier to place a boot on a metal rung, a little practice is all that is needed to feel comfortable standing in webbing.

Here's how I use my etriers: First I place protection, then I attach a carabiner to the protection. Using a separate carabiner, I attach the top of my aid ladder to the carabiner clipped to the protection. I repeat that process, securing etriers for both legs. Now I climb the steps of both ladders until I am standing in the top rungs. From there, I search the wall for a hospitable crack. Finding one, I place another piton, chock, or camming device and attach a carabiner to that protection.

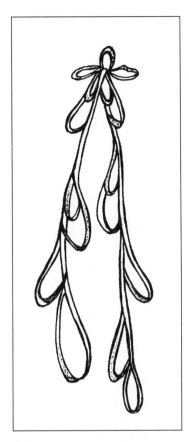

Aiders.

Mike Corbett (loaded down with camming devices, pitons, and other equipment) stands in etriers while reaching to make his next placement.

At this point, there are two options. The more efficient method requires the use of four aiders. When I reach the top steps of the first two ladders, I clip two more to the protection, step onto them, unclip the lower ladders, clip them onto my hardware sling, climb up to the top steps of the new ladders, and repeat the process.

A less efficient method is to climb with only two ladders. That means, however, that when I reach the top steps of both ladders, I have to place all my weight in ladder number one, unclip ladder number two and place it up higher, then stand in ladder number two while I reach down, unclip ladder number one, and move it up the wall. It's an inefficient but less cluttered way to climb. With only two ladders, you have fewer loops of webbing hanging from your body.

You can buy fancy, professionally sewn etriers, or you can make your own out of 20 feet of flat webbing. You should not have to worry about a homemade etrier giving out. The loops are formed with knots, and as you stand on the webbing, the knots tighten. Even if your etriers did give way, you would still be tied in to your protection, precluding a big fall. Having said that, it's still wise to test your homemade ladders near ground level before trying them on a big wall.

I once had a pair of etriers that I really liked. I liked them so much, I kept using them even after they started to fray. Halfway up El Capitan, the rungs ripped out. I fell about 3 feet. It was unnerving and a little embarrassing, but otherwise not a big deal.

Hammers

If you use pitons, you must carry a hammer. For years, the most popular hammer has been the Yosemite by Chouinard. It features a hickory handle, which I still prefer over fiberglass or metal, and a lanyard to prevent your dropping it. The lanyard is long enough to sling over your shoulder, allowing you to reach up high and swing the hammer.

Traditionally, some of the best climbing hammers have been made by Forrest, Colorado Mountain Industries (CMI), A5 Adventures, and Stubai, an Austrian firm. Today, Forrest and CMI are no longer available.

The newer version of the Yosemite hammer has a hole in its head large enough to accept a carabiner. To extract reluctant pitons or copperheads, clip a carabiner to the hammer and a piece of webbing to the carabiner. Clip the other end of the webbing to a second carabiner, which in turn is attached to the eye of, say, a piton. Now give the webbing a good yank; it should whip the piton out of the crack.

Piton hammers (*from top to bottom*): an A5, an Old Stubai from Austria, a Chouinard Yosemite Hammer, and a Salewa from Germany. The Salewa has a metal handle; the rest have handles made of hickory.

Hooks

Hooks, also called *sky hooks* or *cliffhangers,* are U-shaped pieces of metal used to climb blank rock. A hook has a hole through which rope or webbing can be threaded, which in turn is attached to a carabiner. Hooks are placed gently—never tossed—onto flakes, nubbins, or other small irregularities in a rock with no cracks. Hooks can be used for free climbing, but they will not hold much of a fall. They are designed to support your weight until you can place better protection. Sometimes you need to rely on a series of hook placements. If you use hooks continuously for 30 or more feet, you are climbing at A5, the extreme end of the aid spectrum.

I rarely leave a hook behind. Exceptions have occurred, usually when the lip I'm hooking is so good that I can tap the hook down and it will stay in place, and I can use it for bombproof protection. In that case, I would leave the hook on the rock.

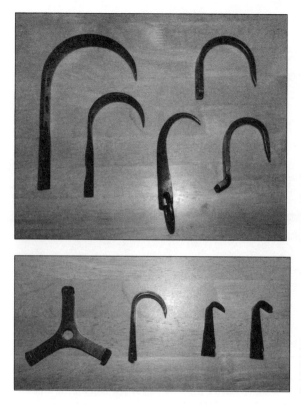

Hooks (*clockwise from top right*): a Captain Hook, a fish hook, a ring angle claw hook, a Mr. Big Stuff hook, and a meat hook.

(*Left to right*): a talon hook, a standard Chouinard hook, a Leeper pointed hook, and a Leeper flat hook.

Bat hooks, invented by Warren Harding, are slightly different, because they are used with a masonry drill bit. The hooks are ground to a point, then tapped or hammered into a shallow (¼-inch) hole manually drilled in the rock.

Ascenders

A rope ascender is a clamp—a mechanical hand, really—that grips a rope without ever letting go or getting tired. It was invented by Swiss bird-watchers in the fifties who needed an easier way to climb trees. Ascenders generally come in pairs—one for each hand.

Ascenders are most commonly used by the second climber, whose job it is to clean the aid pitch. They're also used in the hauling system: A downward-pointing ascender anchored to the rock prevents haul bags from sliding back down.

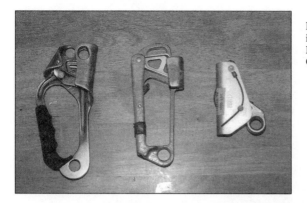

Popular ascenders include (*left to right*) Petzel, Jumar, and Gibbs.

Although Jumar is a brand name for one particular type of ascender (others include Gibbs, Petzel, CMI, and CLOG), it has become synonymous with the act itself. It's common for climbers to say, "I

Mike Corbett using ascenders (one in each hand) to climb a fixed rope. Attached to each ascender is an etrier for the legs.

Mike Corbett using ascenders to provide stability. Corbett keeps his legs and feet shoulder-width apart to prevent himself from falling over to either side.

Corbett rests while using ascenders. The nylon webbing attaching the ascenders to the harness enables a climber to let go of the ascenders to rest and allows the second climber (cleaner) to remove protection.

jumared up to the first ledge," even if they are using a competing brand.

Working on a ratchet principle, ascenders slide up a rope, but when weighted, a cam causes the handle to pinch the rope and stop downward movement. This does minimal damage to the rope, although if you were to use mechanical ascenders over and over on the same rope, it would eventually fray. Realistically, however, ropes wear out for other reasons before that happens.

Most climbers prefer Jumar ascenders, which can be clipped to a rope without taking them apart. The disadvantage of a Jumar is that it tends to slip on icy ropes. The only ascender I know that works well on icy ropes is the Gibbs, but it has to be taken apart every time you want to clip it to a rope. This is so time-consuming that if there is no risk of icy ropes, I opt for Jumars.

Belay Devices

To belay is to pay out rope to the leader from a secure position. If the leader is placing protection, the belayer is smoothly feeding out rope, maintaining enough slack to avoid pulling the leader off the rock. If the leader falls, the belayer has to make sure no more rope feeds out.

There are a number of ways to do this. The oldest and most primitive is the body belay, or hip belay, in which the belayer wraps the rope around his back just above the hips. The "live" end of the rope, the end going to the climber, is gripped in the left hand (guide hand). The right hand (brake hand) holds the rope on the other side of the body. The idea is that the friction caused by the rope traveling around the belayer's body will allow the belayer to gain control of the rope in case the climber falls.

In the past twenty years or so, the body belay has been replaced by several devices designed to enhance that friction without sacrificing human skin. The first and still most popular device is the *Sticht plate*, a 4-ounce disc with a hole in it. A bight of rope is passed through the hole and clipped to a screw-gate carabiner on the harness. During belay, the rope passes through the belay plate, through the carabiner, then back through the belay plate again. The belayer's hands do exactly what they would do during a body belay. The radical bend that the rope makes as it passes through the belay plate creates the friction necessary to hold a fall.

Another device that can be used for belaying is a *figure-eight ring*, so called because it looks like the numeral 8. The goal of increasing friction is the same as for the Sticht plate: The rope is threaded

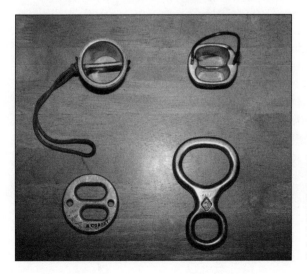

Belay devices include (*clockwise from bottom right*) the figure-eight (also the most popular descender), the Sticht plate, the Lowe Tuber, and the Chouinard Air Traffic Controller.

through the bigger hole of the figure-eight ring, then back through the smaller hole; then it's clipped to a locking carabiner on the climber's harness. The radical turn of the rope creates the friction necessary to control the rope.

Another lightweight choice is the Lowe Tuber, a cone-shaped tube that works on the same principle as the other belay devices. Pass a bight of rope through the tube and clip a locking carabiner to it.

The Munter hitch, introduced to climbing by Swiss climber Werner Munter, requires no hardware save a special carabiner attached to a harness. During a fall, the brake hand moves forward and the hitch locks on itself.

All belay devices are attached to the belayer with a screw-gate (locking) carabiner.

Descenders

Used for rappeling fixed ropes, these devices permit a controlled slide by, you guessed it, creating friction. The original technique was the *Dulfursitz*, also called the *body rappel*, a way of wrapping the rope around your body to create enough friction to slow your descent.

The body rappel has been out of favor for many years. In its place, we have the figure-eight descender and the *carabiner brake*, a configuration of six carabiners arranged so that when a rope is threaded through them, the friction permits a controlled slide. A figure-eight descender is lightweight and easy to use; make sure the one you get is good to at least 3,000 pounds.

To rig the figure-eight, thread the rappel rope through the big hole, then around behind the little hole, and clip to a locking biner. Clip another locking carabiner (or two regular biners, gates reversed) on your harness through the small hole. The friction created by this bend will allow a capable rappeler to control speed of descent.

Webbing

Nylon straps, known as *webbing*, come in two basic styles and have countless uses. One style is the 1-inch tubular webbing used to make *runners*. Runners are loops of webbing approximately 6 feet long tied with a water knot. On a big wall, I carry twelve to twenty runners. They have many different purposes, but the most important one is to control the way the rope runs. To avoid rope drag—excessive resistance—you want the rope running more or less straight, not zigzagging all over the rock. Runners can help you achieve that. Or you might use runners to move the rope away from trouble spots like sharp edges.

If you wanted to use a tree for protection, you might girth-hitch it with a runner. You also could use a runner to tie several anchors together, to equalize anchor points so that you're stressing several instead of just one, or to carry gear slung over your shoulder.

The other type of webbing, called *tie-off loops*, or *hero loops*, are short loops about 2 feet long made of ½-inch or ⁹⁄₁₆-inch tubular webbing and tied with a water knot. If you are unable to drive a piton in all the way, you might girth-hitch such webbing around the piton close to the rock to reduce leverage. Known as "tying off a piton," this is a way of reducing leverage by relocating the pressure point closer to the rock. A hero loop can also be threaded through the eye of a piton, then clipped to the carabiner through which the rope passes. This gives the rope more flexibility.

Bolts

If you can't find a crack to accommodate your protection, you may have to drill a hole in the rock. You will do this manually with a masonry drill bit, either a star drive or a rawl drive—no power drills should be used. The standard hole, ¼ inch in diameter and 1½ inches deep, is created by tapping the drill bit against the rock and twisting. It's not uncommon to take twenty to thirty minutes to achieve this, depending on the sharpness of the drill bits.

When you're finished, the bolt stud you hammer into the hole should be slightly larger than the hole itself to assure snugness.

Attached to the bolt is a *bolt hanger*, a strip of metal with two holes. The smaller hole accommodates the bolt; the larger, a carabiner.

Bolts are permanent—and therefore controversial. They usually are placed only by the first ascent team. It is advisable, however, to carry a bolt kit on a long aid climb; you may have to replace missing bolts or beef up anchors you think are suspect.

Specialty Items

Specialty items are tricky gadgets with names like copperheads, circle heads, mashies, and bashies—little blobs of metal that can be smashed into shallow cracks, maybe nothing more than grooves that won't

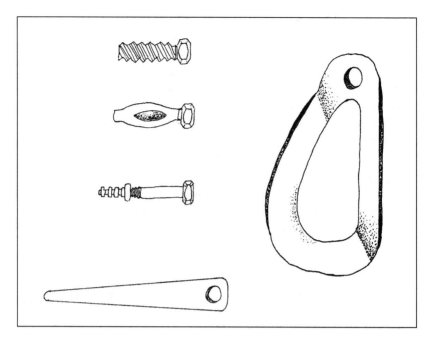

Bolting equipment. The three bolts at the top left of the drawing (*top to bottom:* a machine bolt, a split-shank rawl screw-top, and a taper bolt) range in size from 1 inch to 1½ inches long--the harder the rock, the longer the bolt. The drift pin (*bottom left*) is used to remove the drill bit from the drill holder. The hanger (*right*) is used to attach a carabiner to a rope.

accept a piton, cam, or chock. First you clean out the crack with a chisel or piton, then pound in the malleable metal with the pick end of your hammer. It may only go in ¹/8 to ¼ inch, but if it's placed and tied off correctly, it will hold a climber's body weight.

Pulleys
Pulleys are used only to pull up your extra equipment. The best type is called a Rock Exotica, which has a built-in cam to prevent the load from sliding back down the rock. Most modern pulleys employ a ball-bearing system for a smoother haul. It's a good idea to carry a spare pulley in case you drop one. If that happens, don't forget to yell, "Pulley!!!"

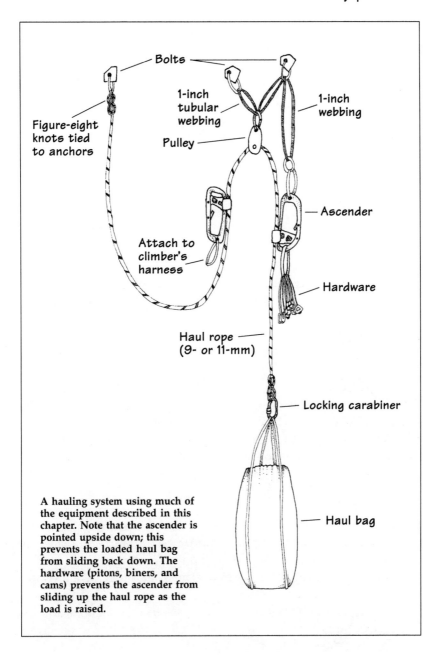

Bolts

1-inch tubular webbing

1-inch webbing

Figure-eight knots tied to anchors

Pulley

Attach to climber's harness

Ascender

Hardware

Haul rope (9- or 11-mm)

Locking carabiner

Haul bag

A hauling system using much of the equipment described in this chapter. Note that the ascender is pointed upside down; this prevents the loaded haul bag from sliding back down. The hardware (pitons, biners, and cams) prevents the ascender from sliding up the haul rope as the load is raised.

– 3 –

Supplies

Besides hard-core equipment, there are plenty of other things to take on a climb, including fluids, food, sleeping gear, clothing, helmet, headlamp, and a first-aid kit.

To carry the gear that is not strapped to your body, you will use haul bags, which resemble army duffel bags but are more abrasion-resistant. For one or two climbers out for a night or two, one haul bag may be enough; if you're out a week or more, two or even three haul bags may be needed. One way to compartmentalize gear, making it easier to find, is to tie daypacks below the haul bags.

When buying haul bags, look for ones with vertical wear straps sewn every few inches for taking the abuse of the rock, and loops on the outside for tying off other equipment.

Fluids

Short of injury, running out of water is the worst thing that can happen to a climbing team. As you probably know, humans can survive much longer without food than without water.

Aid climbing can range from one pitch that may take a couple of hours to thirty pitches that may take ten days or more. The amount of fluids you carry should be based on weather predictions and the number of people-days (number of people times number of days).

On cool days, I recommend 2 quarts per person per day. On moderately hot days, figure a minimum of 3 quarts per person per day. But let's say it's really hot—high eighties to more than a hun-

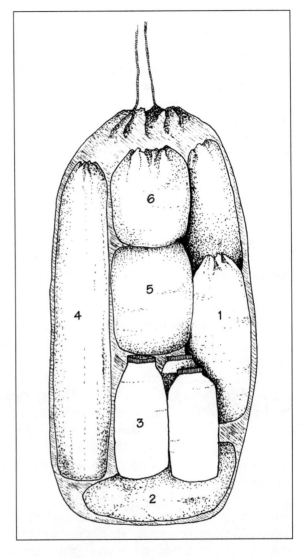

A haul bag packed with sleeping gear (1), rain gear (2), water in plastic bottles (3), a Portaledge (4), food (5), and miscellaneous items (6).

dred—with plenty of exposed granite to reflect heat. You may find fluid needs increasing to nearly 4 quarts a day. If so, a two-person team on a seven-day climb (fourteen people-days) will need a total of 56 quarts, or 14 gallons. Because a gallon of water weighs 8.3 pounds, this team must haul a daunting 116 pounds of water.

I always calculate how much water I think my team needs, and then add a couple of gallons. Somehow that works out just about right. My thinking might run like this: It's a warm seven-day climb with two people. We will probably need 3 quarts daily per person. That's 42 quarts, more than 85 pounds. But can we really make it in seven days? It might take longer. I'd better add a couple of gallons to be sure. If it looks like we're on schedule, we can drink more.

My personal rule is that half my team's water requirement will be satisfied by some type of sports drink. My favorite is Gatorade, but you may prefer one of the other brands. Sports drinks not only provide flavoring that helps cut through unwelcome mouth mung, but they also replace electrolytes, minerals like potassium, magnesium, and sodium that are lost with sweat.

Other drink possibilities: Kool-Aid, Wyler's lemonade, powdered milk, hot chocolate, tea, or coffee. The last three demand a lot of baggage, however, including stove, fuel, canister, and pot. Keep in mind, too, that coffee is a diuretic, causing water loss through urination. Climbers should avoid anything that causes the body to use more water.

I definitely do not recommend sodas, which are too heavy, too sweet, and poor thirst quenchers in the long run. Carbonated drinks in general are unsatisfying when they get warm, not an unreasonable possibility on a rock wall.

Fluids should be stored in small plastic water bottles, not hulking 5-gallon containers. Avoid glass. The bombproof Nalgene 1-quart bottles are ideal. You can also use somewhat larger bleach bottles or restaurant syrup bottles. The risk of carrying water in 5-gallon containers should be obvious: If you spring a leak, you lose a significant amount of water. Your climb, which had been going so well, is suddenly in peril.

So devastating is the loss of even a little water that climbers should take special precautions to ensure that the bottle tops won't loosen. Place some plastic wrap under the cap and screw it down; this acts as a gasket. If you're on a long climb and won't need some of your water for several days, wrap duct tape around the tops of your bottles. Some climbers tape entire bottles for insulation and toughness.

When you pack your water in haul bags, wrap sleeping pads around it for extra insulation and protection. Whether your haul bags are canvas or nylon, the material will wear out quickly if it is pinched between rock and hard water bottles. Moreover, sleeping pads insulate so well that your water, chilled by night, will stay at least cool during hot days.

My first experience running out of water was on a thousand-foot cliff called the Rostrum. The climb is usually done in a few hours, but I decided to make it my first ever overnighter. We took sleeping bags and a haul bag with food and water. But I'd never climbed with my partner before, and we were slow. We ended up spending two nights and running out of water half a day early. I couldn't believe how miserable it was, how slowed we were by deprivation. When we finally got back to a road, I practically tackled the first people I saw for water.

I ran out of water another time, near the top of El Capitan. But I had climbed it a month earlier and stashed a gallon of water near the top. So even though we ran out, we knew that water was there. The psychological value of that knowledge cannot be overstated. Most climbers who run out of water don't know when they'll get their next drink. The uncertainty can be devastating.

When I climbed Half Dome in 1991 with Mark Wellman, we intended to take seven days. Secretly, though, we thought we might do it in five. Instead, we ran into storms, got sick, and took thirteen days to top out. Yet the 12 gallons of water we took was sufficient. In contrast to our hot El Cap climb two years earlier, waiting out storms on Half Dome dramatically reduced our needs. Lying in sleeping bags all day, we needed less food and water. That was fortunate, because the last thing in the world I wanted was for us to be rescued on national television.

Store water in plastic bottles with handles, like bleach and syrup bottles. Tie little loops of webbing to each handle, and then link the loops. Connect the whole lot to the top outside straps of the haul bag, tucking the water bottles inside the haul bag. That way, if you blow out the bottom of your haul bag, you won't lose all your water.

Food

To determine which foods to take, have a chat with your partners. Find out preferences and aversions, though this is neither the time nor the place for finicky eaters. If there are no objections, emphasize sturdy foods like bagels, salami, energy bars, gorp, dried fruit, breakfast bars, Pop-Tarts, chewy fruit snacks, hard candies, and some canned goods, such as fruit, chili, and my favorite, beans and franks, affectionately known as "beanie weenies." I like cheese and have long taken white cheeses (without refrigeration, orange cheese becomes an oily mess), but I have recently learned that cheese takes a lot of water to digest. If this is true, cheese is a bad idea.

Most foods taken backpacking can be used for climbing. I'm sure that just about anything edible has been taken on one climb or another. As evidence, I offer the case of a friend whose partners sent him out to do the shopping for their climb. He came back from the grocery store and loaded up the haul bags. His partners were unaware of what he had bought. Six hundred feet up the rock, they decided to spend the night on a small ledge. They pulled out their rations, and lo!—they had a sack of potatoes and some beer. Suds and spuds. I can only surmise that my friend figured, "Ah, potatoes— these will last a long time!" He was right, of course. Without a stove, they were destined to last forever.

I have a highly scientific method of shopping for a climb. For two people doing a seven-day climb, I fill up one grocery cart. I figure one grocery cart will last two people a long time. When I get home, I spread everything out on a ground cloth and divide it into days. Seven days, seven piles. I imagine each person's meals; better yet, I write it down. Do we have enough? If there are gaping holes, I return to the grocery store and fill them.

I don't recommend taking a stove. Even a little backpacking stove weighs quite a bit, and that's only the beginning. You must also bring fuel, fuel container, pot, and possibly extra water. Your haul bags are already heavy and bulky. Think about it.

In fifty El Capitan climbs, I've taken a stove only twice. One time we decided to try hot meals for a change; the other time was when I climbed with Warren Harding, who was sixty-five at the time. He insisted on having a stove so that he could bathe his brandy in hot chocolate.

Harding had a butane stove with a screw-on fuel cartridge. If you are determined to carry a stove, I recommend the cartridge type to eliminate messing with fuel.

Repackage most foods in Ziploc bags. If the product is sold in a box, toss the box and bag the food. Organize food into stuff sacks and then store in haul bags, insulated with jackets and sweaters. Keep it near the water for limited refrigeration. At meal times, take out what you need, then reseal quickly. The dry mountain air will desiccate food in a hurry.

Don't forget the utensils. You need a knife and a spoon, but maybe not a fork. A good Swiss army knife will supply blade, can opener, tweezers, and scissors for first aid, even a toothpick for after-dinner dental needs.

Sleeping Equipment

I guess if I qualify as an expert in any subject, it is sleeping on big walls. On El Capitan alone, I have spent 187 nights, half a year of my life.

Rule number one is this: If there's the slightest chance you might have to spend a night on a wall, take a sleeping bag. There are numerous brands, but only two basic choices of fill: down or synthetic. I have both types, but when I climb, I leave the down bag at home. Both are plenty warm, but synthetic fill has one overwhelming advantage: If it gets wet, it won't lose all its heat-retaining power. Wet down, on the other hand, is about as useless on a climb as gaiters. If your down bag gets drenched, it has no chance of drying out on that climb. It will weigh a ton, and you can't wring it out. You might as well toss it off the cliff.

I prefer a tapered mummy bag with a hood; it allows me to batten down the hatches and leave only my face exposed.

On a rock wall, there are three reasonable choices for places to sleep: on a ledge, a portable ledge, or a hammock.

No matter which one you choose, you will need a sleeping pad to defend against the cold gnawing at you from below. The best sleeping bag in the world will be ineffective without a pad.

Sleeping on a ledge requires no equipment beyond bag, pad, and the usual anchors. Don't ever sleep on a ledge without protection, lest you discover that your lifelong nightmare of plunging through space has finally come true. A good ledge is not without its advantages: It feels secure, and it allows climbers to lay out gear, take inventory, and pack efficiently the next morning.

In the absence of a real rock ledge, the most comfortable alternative is a portable ledge, a cotlike sleeping platform that is suspended from the rock by multiple anchors. Introduced to climbers in the late seventies, the portable ledge has a rectangular frame made out of poles of tubular aluminum. The poles fit together and pull apart like tent poles, making it collapsible and portable. Nylon is stretched around the poles, which are in sleeves. In each corner are webbing straps that allow this cot to be suspended from a single point. The straps are adjustable so that you can compensate for the angle of the rock and make your bed level.

If you climb with a significant other, you should know that they sell double-wide portable ledges. Rain flies are available to cover both singles and doubles; when it is secured, the appearance is of a pup tent hanging off the side of a rock. The beauty of a portable ledge is that it offers a good night's sleep. Some climbers take one even if ledges are available. They are comfortable and sturdy—and expensive. As of this writing, portable ledges sell for $400 to $600, depending on the model.

If you can't buy or borrow a portable ledge, a last resort is a hammock. This is not the sort of hammock you sling between two trees. A climber's hammock has six straps that pyramid to a single point from which it hangs. The effect is somewhat akin to sleeping in a potato sack. Climbing hammocks are fairly cheap, lightweight, and miserably uncomfortable. A rain fly fits over the hammock (don't forget to seal the seams), but if it pours, you can count on getting wet. Despite the disadvantages, climbers facing only one bivouac will often carry a hammock, choosing to endure one bad night in exchange for less weight. Mountain Tools makes a good hammock for about $100.

By 1979, anyone interested in big walls was familiar with portable ledges. In fact, that year I made my own portable ledge out of aluminum poles from the hardware store. My girlfriend, Lisa, was good with a sewing machine, and I was good with a hacksaw. I cut up the poles and put them together with bungee cords. I like to say that she made the bed and I lay on it—twice successfully on El Capitan.

Clothing

Clothing decisions will be based largely on the season of the year and the duration of the climb. Choosing which clothes to take is easier in the summer, when it is usually warmer and drier, but even then it's important to make the right decisions.

If you climb in shorts, they should be durable with a reinforced seat. If you favor long pants, they should be light in color, durable, and baggy. Several companies make pants that qualify, but the most popular among climbers seems to be Gramicci. Whether you wear shorts or not, you may want knee pads, especially if you're doing a lot of hanging belays that cause your knees to bang against the rock. Although elbow pads are not popular, knee pads are *de rigueur* among some climbers.

I recommend a long-sleeved T-shirt to prevent sunburned arms, though you should still apply sunscreen to other exposed parts of your body. A baseball cap will protect your head, but it causes heat retention. A visor lets some heat out but leaves the top of the head vulnerable. A foreign-legion-style hat with flaps will shield your sensitive neck, but it, too, holds in heat. The one thing we can agree on: Good sunglasses with wraparound protection are essential to safeguard your eyes from harmful ultraviolet rays.

I like to carry a bandanna for use as both a headband and a neckerchief. On hot days, I'll soak it in water. It dries out quickly, but I'm left with a headband that helps prevent sweat from running into my eyes.

I strongly urge you to take foul-weather gear, regardless of month or forecast. It weighs little and is too important to leave behind. Because of the unpredictable nature of mountain weather, you should take the following even in summer: pile jacket and sweater, rain jacket and pants, wool cap, and gloves or mittens. In June 1982, I started a ten-day climb of El Capitan in oppressive heat. Near the end of the climb, it began to snow. That's how quickly the weather can change. At the start of the climb, heat was the enemy; by the end, cold and wet played that role. Survival meant being prepared for both.

In the winter, much more is riding on these decisions. A mistake could be fatal. Although you may still wear little while climbing in winter, you will need multiple layers as soon as the exercise stops. I recommend warm socks, polypropylene underwear, pile pants and jacket, a Gore-Tex or coated nylon rain suit, top to bottom, and a pile or wool cap. In the winter, I always carry two caps, two pairs of gloves, extra capelene socks, a sweater, and overmitts. I stash the clothes I'm not wearing in large Ziploc bags. That way, if rainwater is running into the haul bags, the clothes are safe. This is critical, because wearing wet clothes, even when the temperature is well above freezing, dramatically increases your risk of hypothermia.

Helmet

Hard head protectors are worn for two main reasons. One is to protect climbers from loose rock falling from above. A rock that broke my finger on El Capitan probably would have killed me if it had struck my helmetless head. On the other hand, a softball-size rock that has reached terminal velocity before it strikes will probably break your helmet. How will your head fare? I haven't yet run that test.

The second important reason to wear a helmet is for protection in case of a fall. Suppose you take a 15-foot fall where the rock is not vertical. This is not a long drop, but on the way down your feet could catch on a projection, flipping you upside down. You could easily hit your head, in which case a helmet would certainly help.

Helmets also offer tangential advantages, like heat retention in the winter and a good place to display your sponsor's logos.

Some climbers continue to resist wearing a helmet: "If I have a bad accident, a helmet's not going to help," you often hear. It's a fatuous argument used to justify what the arguer wants to do. Others will complain that helmets are too confining. But the truth is, once you get used to a helmet, you don't even notice it. It just becomes another piece of rock-climbing equipment.

A few years ago, the slogan among climbers could have been "Wear a helmet, be a geek." No more. Criticism of climbers who choose to wear helmets is sparse. Stars like Jim Bridwell or Peter Croft aren't going to get on someone for wearing a helmet, because they too have worn helmets at one time or another.

Even I have taken to wearing a helmet. In my youth, I usually climbed without one. I was lucky, but now I have a young daughter and feel I should take every precaution. It's reckless to climb without a helmet, and I was guilty of being reckless. It's another example of "do as I say, not as I used to do."

Headlamp

Lamps that strap onto head or hat will keep your hands free for other tasks. Don't even think about climbing with a flashlight or, worse, with no light at all. You may need artificial light for those times you want to start early or finish late. Or let's say you climb all you can during the day and then have to make camp after dark. You will need a headlamp to find equipment and places to sleep.

I prefer to stop when it's light, set up camp, and then, if I still have energy, climb past the bivouac. When I'm done, I set a fixed rope and rappel right down into my bed.

I recommend that each climber have his own headlamp, complete with new batteries in the lamp and an extra set stashed elsewhere. Even then, use your lamp only when necessary. You don't know when you might need it for hours at a time.

Petzl makes the headlamp that is the overwhelming favorite among climbers. It is a single lightweight unit—no separate battery pack, no wires to get tangled.

First-Aid Kit

I confess that I have usually carried only a minimal first-aid kit. There are dozens of items you could include in a complete kit, but how can you know which ailment will befall you? At a minimum, you should carry aspirin or some other pain reliever, adhesive tape, gauze, Band-Aids, and antiseptic cream. I rely on the tweezers and scissors from my Swiss army knife to complete the kit.

Only once in my nineteen years of climbing did I feel poorly prepared for an injury I received. My partner, about 100 feet above me, put a piton in a crack, and a big chunk of rock broke off into his lap. As big as a case of beer, it probably weighed 60 pounds. My partner tried to throw it off to the side as far as he could, but the rock shattered, and a piece headed directly for me at terminal velocity. It hit me on the hand, cutting it in several places and breaking the second metacarpal, the bone directly below the index finger. The force of the blow flipped me upside down and sent me into shock.

So there I was with a smashed, bleeding hand and no first-aid kit. We had two pitches to go before we reached any kind of decent ledge. There was nothing to do but try to gut it out. I put a mitten over the injured hand, figuring that if it was out of sight, it was out of mind. At the very least, it kept me from conjuring up visions of amputation.

I discovered that I was able to jumar with one hand. Upon reaching the ledge, we found a piece of wood and made a splint. Then we took duct tape off the water bottles and wrapped it around the splint. That was our first-aid kit. You, who are smarter, should take a more complete kit. After that experience, I upgraded my medical supplies.

– 4 –

Getting Started

So you've decided you're going to further your climbing skills. You're going to step beyond free climbing into sixth class. You have your eyes on a piece of rock that can be climbed only with aid techniques. Where do you begin?

First you need to determine what gear you need. I suggest you start out on a route that permits you to use the equipment you already have. If you are a free climber, you probably have a rack of hexes, stoppers, carabiners, camming devices, and your own rope. If so, the only gear you immediately need is a pair of etriers, which you can make or buy, and some ascenders, which you can probably borrow. In other words, don't spend a lot of money on aid gear until you find out if you really like it.

Try to befriend some aid climbers who can give you advice and lend you equipment. You might try aid-climbing a free climb you already know. If you clean-climb—that is, without a hammer—nobody will be offended by your aid-climbing a short free climb to get the feel of the aiders.

Aid classifications range from A1, the easiest, to A5, the most difficult. Start your aid-climbing career on an A1 crack. A1 means that you can trust all the equipment you put in the rock. It's a nice, deep, secure crack, and every piece of protection will hold not only your body weight, but also a fall if you make a mistake.

If you can't find an experienced partner, at least find someone to belay you. You need someone who's patient, who knows how to belay, and who doesn't mind sitting a spell while you fumble your way up your first aid crack.

Rookie aid climbers need to pace themselves, moving piece by piece up the cliff. Each time you put in a piece of protection, you attach your aid ladders to that piece, move to the top step, place another piece of protection in the rock, reattach your aid ladders to it, clip your rope to the carabiner attached to that protection—and just keep repeating the process.

In the past, as a free climber, you've always relied on the natural handholds and footholds of the rock, so aid climbing is bound to feel foreign to you. You're not used to aid ladders, which are about 5 feet long and full of loops, with a maddening tendency to flap in the wind and get tangled with each other.

With patience, you will work through that. After two pitches of aid climbing, you should have gained the feel of the equipment. From there, you can progress quickly.

Try to learn as much as you can about the sport. Do some research. Read books. Good guidebooks are very helpful, providing information—maybe even drawings—on just about every climb in your area. They will tell you everything from whether there's a pendulum to how many rurps to take. What they won't tell you is how much food, water, and time to take. The climb's grade will give you a rough idea of its duration, but it's the skills of the climbing team that will ultimately decide how long the team is on the rock.

In any guidebook, you will see a grading system that reflects the length of climbs.

Grade 1: Couple of hours

Grade 2: About half a day

Grade 3: Most of a day

Grade 4: All day, maybe overnight

Grade 5: One night out

Grade 6: More than one night out

This is different from "class," which measures the difficulty of a climb. A route can be Grade 6 (multiple nights out), A3 (aid difficulty), and 5.10 (most difficult free climbing).

Keep in mind that because climbers are not all created equal, one person's Grade 4 might be another's Grade 5. For example, almost all the routes on El Capitan and Half Dome are Grade 6, but many of them can be done by very skilled climbers in a day.

Talk to experienced climbers. Ask them how they learned to aid-climb and where they climbed initially. Did they find aid climbing difficult? How long did it take them to get the hang of it? Ask their advice on whether you should buy pitons and when and where it is appropriate to use those pitons. Should you have hooks? Copperheads? Ask them how you can advance to the next level.

When you probe other climbers, make the last question "Do you know another climber I could talk to?" That's called networking, an important learning tool.

The answers you receive from experienced aid climbers will probably encourage you. Most will tell you that aid climbing was hard at first. Intimidating, too, but ultimately very rewarding. Because in aid climbing, you are repeatedly testing your protection. Ninety-nine percent of the time in free climbing, you don't find out if your protection will hold; not so in aid climbing, a sport in which each piece of protection must prove its worth by supporting your weight.

The only way to improve as an aid climber is to keep challenging yourself with progressively more difficult climbs. Work up through A2, A3, A4, and A5, doing multipitch aid routes.

For many aid climbers, the ultimate goal is a big wall. A big wall provides ten to thirty pitches of aid experience. And if you don't know a lot about aid climbing after thirty pitches, you may never know. After one big wall, most people are pretty competent aid climbers. The sky's the limit after that.

– 5 –

Technique

Technique will take the aid climber much farther than brute strength and determination, although it's nice to have all three. Substituting physical power for technique results in sloppy climbing and quickly depletes energy. The result may be retreat or failure.

Technique means using your body and equipment efficiently and properly. If you can accomplish this, you will likely be a safe and successful climber. Use of proper technique also allows novice climbers to advance their skills more rapidly. So take your time and learn how to do each procedure correctly the first time, because bad habits are hard to break.

Rope Management

Because the rope is the single most important piece of climbing equipment, it's imperative that you take care of it. Besides keeping it clean, you have to avoid kinks and knots by careful coiling or by using a rope bag. Rope management is especially critical for the belayer, who must feed out the rope smoothly to the leader.

One method is called *pooling*, laying one end of the rope on the ground, then piling it carefully in concentric loops. In this way, the top of the pile should feed out smoothly without kinks or knots. Avoid dirt by putting your backpack on the ground and then piling your rope on top of it. Be sure to keep track of both ends of the rope.

Another method is known as *lap coiling*, in which you feed the rope through a loop of webbing—a runner—to help keep it organized.

Probably your best option is a rope bag. Stuff your rope in the bag, carry it to the climb, and enjoy a clean feed once you're there.

Rope management is far more than an obsession with neatness— at times, it's a matter of life or death. Belayers with rope problems must be able to solve them without pulling the lead off the rock.

After the climb, you must recoil your ropes. I sit down and loop the rope around a knee and a foot, making big coils. Then I take the last 5 or 6 feet of rope and wrap it repeatedly around the loops to keep them in place. You can also make a mountaineer's coil, in which you form loops and use leftover rope to make shoulder straps and a waist belt. You can wear it like a backpack—if you don't already have a backpack.

Belaying. The two principal belaying activities are paying out the rope to the leader and stopping the rope from paying out if the leader falls. It's not often you literally have someone else's life in your

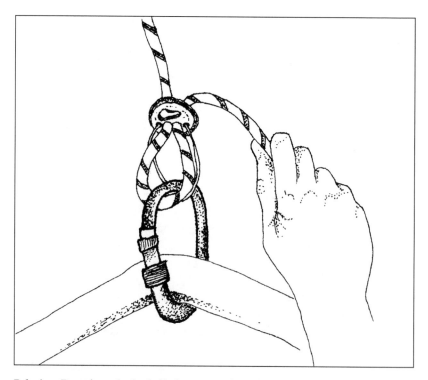

Belaying: Rope from the lead climber passes through a Sticht plate; a locking carabiner then links the rope with the belayer's harness, after which the rope passes back through the Sticht plate and on to the belayer's brake hand.

hands, but belaying is one of those times. Most climbers, realizing its deadly importance, become conscientious belayers.

Once upon a time, before belay devices, there was the body belay. In the body belay, the rope is wrapped around the back at the waist. The left hand, called the *guide hand*, feeds the rope to the leader; the right hand, known as the *brake hand*, never leaves the rope, fingers clenched at the ready. To stop a fall, the brake hand yanks the rope toward the left hip. Belayers must be alert, ready to react at the first sign of trouble.

The body belay is the riskiest way to belay. Friction is created by the belayer's body, so there's a risk of rope burns on the back and hands. Today most climbers create friction with a belay device, such as a Sticht plate or a figure-eight, allowing them to lock the rope tight in case of a fall.

The same rules apply with a belay device as with a body belay. In both cases, the belay is controlled by a guide hand and a brake hand, and the brake hand never leaves the rope.

It's critical that the lines of communication remain open between belay and lead. If there are any problems, the belayer should notify the lead immediately. Of course, it helps if lead and belay are speaking the same language. About a dozen basic signals enable climbers to say what needs to be said:

"On belay?" says the climber before starting.

"Belay on," replies the belayer when ready.

"Climbing," says the leader before starting.

"Climb," responds the belayer when ready to belay.

"Up rope," says the leader wanting the slack pulled in.

"Slack," says the leader wanting the belayer to let out rope.

"Tension," says the leader wanting the belayer to hold him
    tight.

"Rock!" shouts the leader when loose rock is falling.

"Watch me!" says the leader feeling especially vulnerable.

"Falling!" says the leader feeling even more vulnerable.

"Belay off," says the climber after anchoring himself.

"Off belay," replies the belayer indicating the belay has ended.

"Rope," says the leader indicating a rope is being dropped.

Placements

Putting anchors in the rock is at the heart of aid climbing. Here are a few tips on how to make the basic placements.

Nuts. For the placement of chocks, hexentrics, and stoppers, I search the rock for gaps and search the gaps for tiny irregularities. Since a nut has to be able to hold a downward pull, I want the down side of the crack to bottleneck, to be smaller than the nut. Wedged in that part of the crack, it shouldn't pull out. The beauty of this type of placement is that it will hold a fall while doing no damage to the rock.

Hexentrics, depending on how they're turned, offer several different configurations. That means a single hex can work in different-size cracks.

Stoppers and hexentrics are great in expanding cracks because you do no hammering. They're also perfect for the bottom of piton scars. Repeated piton use opens up the top of a crack, but down at the bottom, where it narrows, it's receptive to hexes and stoppers.

A bomber stopper placement in a bottlenecking crack. Pulling down on a stopper during placement should prevent it from lifting out unexpectedly.

Spring-Loaded Camming Devices. Ideally, SLCDs should be placed so that all the cams are touching the rock surface inside the crack. You can place them so that only two cams are touching rock, and they will probably hold your body weight until you can put in better protection; however, don't count on those two cams to hold a fall.

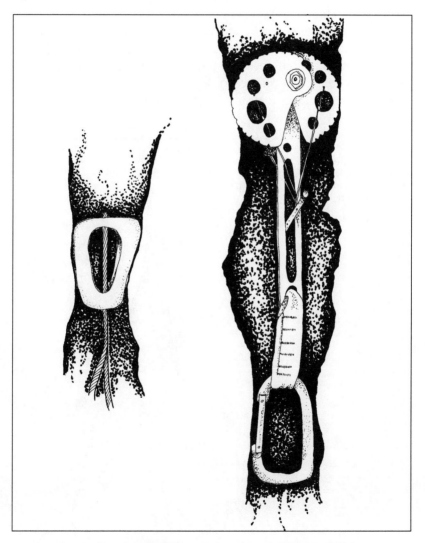

A stopper in a bottleneck crack (*left*), and a properly placed SLCD (*right*).

Align the stem in the direction of pull. Try not to offset the cams, as that diminishes the holding power. Avoid a tipped placement, with the cams wide open. Ideally, the cams should be positioned at midrange.

Avoid rocking the cam tips. Clip your rope to a sling long enough to ensure that you won't move the SLCD as you climb past it. Don't cram an oversize SLCD into an undersize placement; it may make removal difficult or impossible.

The advantage of a camming device is that the more weight you put on it, the more it expands and grips the crack. I've twice had cams pull out, but only because I hadn't set them properly. The inside of the crack was composed of loose flakes, so I had the SLCD wedged against flakes instead of solid rock. But that's two mistakes

In "tying off short" 9/16-inch tubular webbing is used to tie off a piton to reduce leverage.

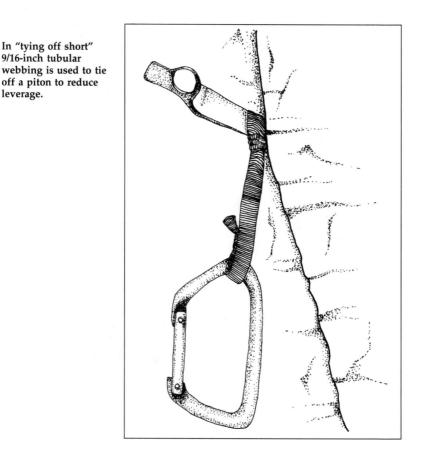

in thousands of placements, and in both cases I tested first by attaching my etriers and giving a tug. If you pay attention to detail, you needn't worry about camming devices pulling out. My recommendation is that anytime you can use an SLCD, do so.

Pitons. If you can't find a spot for a nut or a cam, you will probably choose a piton. They come in a wide range of sizes to fit cracks both thick and thin. Pitons share a common trait: When hammered in properly, all except the tiny rurp make a high-pitch ringing sound, almost bell-like. If you hear more of a dull thud, chances are the placement is insecure. Regardless of pitch, give the placement a tug, then a bounce; if it seems secure, check if it will hold your body weight before counting on it to hold a fall.

If a piton won't go in a crack very far, you can tie a short piece of nylon webbing, called a *tie-off loop* or a *hero loop*, to the piton near the rock. Known as "tying off short," this technique reduces leverage, effectively placing less weight on the questionable piton.

Hooks. Hooks are appropriate for tiny ledges and flakes that will accommodate no other protection short of bolts. Hooks are innately precarious, designed to hold body weight, not falls. The best tech-

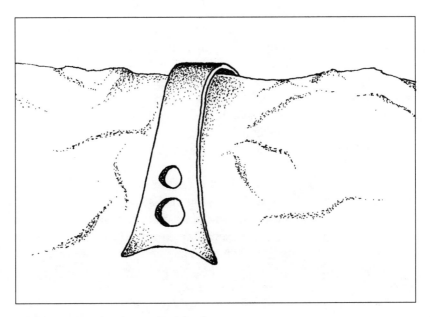

A bomber hook placed over a lip of rock.

nique is to position the hook carefully and give it a tug before trusting it with your body weight.

Copperheads. A copperhead is basically a blob of soft metal with an attached loop of cable for clipping to a carabiner. Before the blob can be hammered into the rock, you must clean the crack. Take a Lost Arrow piton and hammer it lightly into the crack. It won't go in very far, but it will chip away rotten, loose rock, leaving a hospitable pocket for a copperhead.

Insert the copperhead and tap it with the blunt end of your hammer until it conforms to the shape of the pocket you formed. Clip a carabiner to the copperhead's wire loop and an etrier to the carabiner.

This creates a precarious hold that will support body weight only; don't count on it to hold a fall. Maybe a copperhead only advances you a couple of feet, but if it helps you find a better placement, it did the job. I've had to put in as many as thirty copperheads in a row, knowing full well that if I made a mistake, I'd zipper them all.

Cleaning Protection

Chocks. Removing, or cleaning, chocks can be a challenge, especially if they've held a fall. Even without a fall, a chock is asked to withstand the downward pull of your equipment and body weight. Standing in your etriers and pulling down on that nut, which is probably softer than the rock, will set it quite well.

To remove a chock, first try lifting it out in the opposite direction from which it went in. Climb above the chock and yank in an upward direction. Still stuck? Wiggle it, or tap it with a carabiner. Don't use a hammer on a chock unless absolutely necessary, because it will deform the chock, possibly ruining it.

If that doesn't work, take out your nut tool, a thin, 9-inch piece of metal that looks like an old ruler with notches in it, giving you more possibilities when you're prying at the nut.

If you are still stymied, you can place a Lost Arrow piton against the nut and tap it with a hammer in an upward direction. Remember to tie on everything you're working with. If you have a Lost Arrow in one hand and a hammer in the other, you will lose an unconnected chock when it pops out.

Camming Devices. Cams are usually easy to remove. Squeezing the trigger reduces the profile, which should permit easy extraction.

Sometimes, though, a cam can be stubborn, especially if it's been extended to the maximum. Once in a while, it will move within a crack after you've climbed past it. Rope drag is the culprit, causing the cam to wiggle up and down—called *walking*—and making it hard even to reach it. If that's your problem, you probably need a tool called a Friend of a Friend. This extender fits onto the stem of a Friend, allowing you to reach farther into the crack than you could with your fingers.

Pitons. Pitons can be the toughest cleaning problems. The first step is to try to loosen the piton by hammering it up and down. Hammer it down as far as you can, then turn the hammer and pound it back up to its limit. Do that back and forth a few times until you feel it loosen.

If it remains defiant, use a "cleaner beener." Clip a junk carabiner to the piton, attach a piece of webbing to it, and attach the webbing to your climbing harness. As you hammer the piton up and down, your weight pulls on it, making removal more likely. And when it finally pops, you won't lose it.

You can also put the pick end of your hammer through the eye of the piton and use the added leverage to pry it out over your shoulder. To prevent the piton from flying off behind you, keep one hand on the hammer and the other on the piton.

Hooks. Since hooks aren't hammered into the rock, there isn't much cleaning to do. They are accessible and should be removed.

Copperheads. Copperheads can usually be whipped out using the following technique: Clip a carabiner to the eye of the copperhead cable. Then attach the carabiner to the head of your hammer. Some hammers have holes to accommodate a carabiner; in the absence of a hole, girth-hitch a short piece of webbing around the hammer handle close to the head. In a backhanded motion, whip the hammer away from your face and jerk that copperhead out.

No go? As a last resort, you can chisel the rock around the copperhead; but if you have to chisel rock, you should rethink the whole idea of removing the copperhead. It's probably better to leave it, because it doesn't take many climbers with chisels to turn a slender crack into a gaping wound. Copperheads are good for only one or two placements anyway, and if you leave them in, someone else will probably use them. How will the next climbers know if they're solid? By running the tug test, followed by the bounce test.

Leading

You must be in peak mental shape to lead a pitch, never mind a climb. The safety of the whole party is entrusted to the leader, who's also the most vulnerable member of the team. One mistake—misjudging loose rock, protection pulling out—puts the whole climb in jeopardy.

The climbing team goes nowhere without its leader. The leader is responsible for at least the next 165 feet, a burden to be taken seriously. It's important that the leader feel confident that he can accomplish the task. Lacking that confidence, a leader has two choices: relinquish the lead or fake it. A tentative, uncertain leader can damage the morale of the whole team. After all, the leader is seeing the climb up close, and if he's not providing good reports, it puts everybody in a funk.

Beneath this veneer of confidence, the leader has to perform. The first rule is to be sure of placements. Since the leader takes the fall in case of a bad placement, he has every reason to be careful. My personal corollary to rule number one is that when you're leading, you can do anything ethical to assure yourself that you're not going to fall. Sometimes you need more assurance than other times.

Say you've just passed a nerve-racking A4 face, when you reach a good, healthy crack. It would be understandable if you whaled on a piton and buried it more than necessary. Yes, it's excessive. And it may be hard for your partner to remove that piton, but the leader is calling the shots. It's his life on the line if anything goes wrong.

Falling

The best advice I can give about falling is to try not to do it. If you must fall, do it on steep rock, where there's less chance that you'll hit anything. One of the biggest dangers is tripping on nonvertical rock, flipping upside down, and hitting your head. Obviously, your best defense there is to wear a helmet.

You have to play a delicate mental game with falling. On the one hand, you should know what you will hit if you do fall; on the other hand, you don't want to dwell on the possibility so much that it distracts you and actually causes a fall. Be ready for the unexpected.

In 1986, I unexpectedly had a hook pull, which resulted in a 15-foot fall. The fall itself was insignificant, but I broke my finger when it became wedged between the rock and a carabiner. It remains my worst climbing injury.

Another time, while climbing an expanding flake, I expanded the flake too much with a piton, and the stopper I was standing on pulled out. Five more pieces followed, and I fell 50 feet, my longest drop ever. Fortunately it happened on rock steeper than 90 degrees, so I didn't hit anything. I wasn't physically hurt, but I was emotionally barren. I was suddenly overcome by a desire to see what was on television.

Where to Place Protection

Deciding where to place protection is a tug-of-war between the available and the possible. Questions abound. How big is the crack? Will it accept a camming device, my first choice? How about my second choice, a stopper? The only times I won't use a cam or a stopper are when a crack is so thin it's suitable only for a rurp or a knife blade or when it's more hole than crack, suitable only for a larger piton.

It's important to remember that you don't have to place the next piece of protection as high as you can reach. You might put in the next piece only a couple of feet above the previous piece, especially if it's the most secure place available. You may only gain a couple of feet, but so what? At least it moves you a little higher, where you can get a better look at what's above.

The lead climber is making constant judgments about which placement will best keep him from falling. He wants the best possible protection, so that even if he errs farther up the rock, this one definitely will stop a fall.

Natural Anchors. Natural anchors are objects to which you might anchor that no climber put in the rock. For example, you might girth-hitch to a tree if it's strong enough to hold you, or you might tie on to a knob of rock, called a *chickenhead*, always making certain it will take a downward pull.

You can also loop webbing over a horn or flake, but be sure it's not a detached flake. Test by tugging. On rare occasions, you can find little rock tunnels, through which you can string webbing and attach protection.

Using Runners

Runners are loops of tubular nylon webbing about 6 feet long that are used to prevent rope drag on climbs that veer or zigzag up a rock. If the rope doesn't run in a straight line, the leader is fighting not only gravity and the weight of the equipment, but also resistance from the rope that seems to want to pull him off the rock. Well-placed runners will reguide the rope so that it runs in a fairly straight line.

Sometimes you can't fix the problem with runners. If you're zigging and zagging all over the rock and can't completely overcome rope drag, then at least be more patient. There's no point in yelling at your partner—he's probably feeding the rope as smoothly as pos-

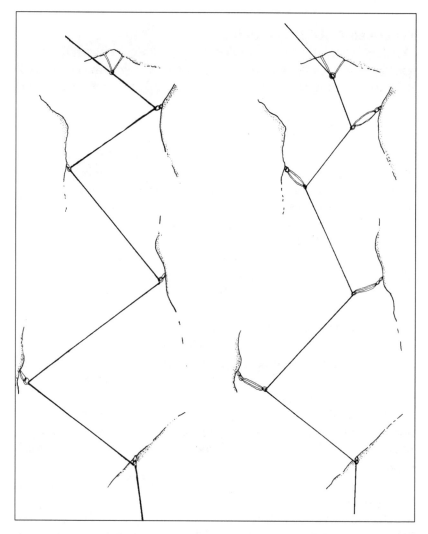

Runners, loops of tubular nylon webbing, help to reduce drag and make a rope run more smoothly as it zigzags up a rock.

sible. If you have to yell, aim your wrath at the route or your equipment. Guidebooks will forewarn you of zigzagging routes and help you pick equipment. I carry ten to fifteen runners on most climbs.

Route Finding

When doing a route previously climbed, getting lost is seldom a problem. Again, guidebooks can provide great clues for finding your way. Also look for traces left by other climbers—piton scars, discarded equipment, smooth rock, lichen scraped away. If someone has climbed a route, he certainly has left behind traces, especially on an aid climb where a new anchor is set every few feet.

Old routes are especially obvious. Climbers doing difficult aid climbs in the fifties and sixties relied exclusively on pitons, which left scars that continue to guide climbers today.

It's valuable to have an idea where a route goes so that you can determine which equipment to carry. Say you climb up 50 feet and the route rounds a bend; only then do you realize that the crack is too wide for the anchors you brought. That's when you're glad you have a second rope, making it easier to send down for more equipment.

Rappeling

If Hollywood movies were to be believed, speed rappeling is a sport in its own right. Actually, rappeling is a controlled means of sliding down a rope that is used after you have completed or abandoned a climb, in preparation for cleaning a pitch, or in the evening after you have climbed above your bivouac.

Historically called *roping down*, the favored technique until recently was the Dulfursitz, or body, rappel. It's the only method that uses no mechanical devices besides a rope. Friction to slow the descent is created by the rope rubbing against your body. The obvious potential for pain during a body rappel was undoubtedly a catalyst in the creation of mechanical descenders. Today the body rappel is as obsolete as the button shoe. It is strictly a survival skill, used only when no other gadgets are available. Still, you should learn how to perform a body rappel in case of emergency. First, face the anchors and straddle the rock. Then bring the rope around behind you, across one hip, up across the chest like a bandolier, over the shoulder, and down the back.

After the body rappel came the carabiner brake, a configuration

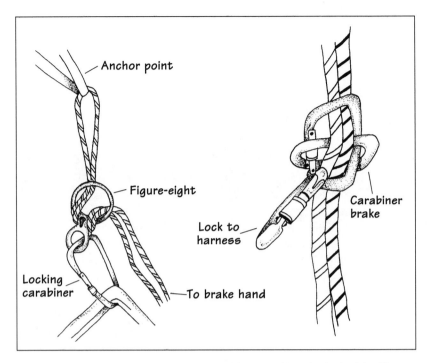

Anchor point

Figure-eight

Lock to harness

Carabiner brake

Locking carabiner

To brake hand

In rappeling, a properly placed figure-eight (*left*) or carabiner brake (*right*) will create enough friction to slow a climber's descent.

of six carabiners attached to the climbing harness and positioned so that when a rope is threaded through them, enough friction is created to slow a descent.

The carabiner brake will still work, but it has been replaced by simpler gadgets, most notably the figure-eight and the *tuberz*, both of which work on the principle that if you bend a rope with enough angle, you will create the friction necessary to slow descent.

Even though rappel devices have made the job easier, you should still be vigilant before and during a rappel. It is arguably the most dangerous part of the climb. Make sure hair and clothing are well clear of the friction device and incapable of becoming entangled.

The scariest part of the rappel is usually the start, especially if you have to go over a lip. Once the rope is weighted, keep the feet planted about shoulder width, and let out some rope until you are leaning well back. Begin the rappel by backpedaling. Stability is increased when you keep the legs spread about shoulder width and nearly perpendicular to the wall. If you drop your feet too far, they will skid off, slamming you against the wall. Twist your upper torso toward your brake hand, and you will be able to look down.

Rappel Tips

1. When learning to rappel, top ropes are safest.
2. Be tied into the belay when sorting out ropes.
3. Make sure anchors are safe.
4. Make sure other climbers are ready before you drop ropes down to them.
5. Tie knots in the ends of the ropes to ensure that you won't slide off the end.
6. Lower rope ends gently to avoid dislodging rocks or tangling ropes.
7. Make sure the ropes reach the bottom of the next belay stance.
8. Rappel as smoothly as possible to avoid cutting the rope or dislodging rocks.
9. After the rappel, remember which rope end has to be pulled to retrieve the rope, lest the knots jam.
10. Give a clear signal when untied from the rope, and move out of the way of the next rappeler.
11. Make sure knots have been untied for retrieval.

Knots
There are several basic knots used in climbing. The advantage of knots over more permanent ways of joining ropes and cords together—like sewn slings—is that knots can be easily untied and retied. The disadvantage is that they weaken the rope. Using knots repeatedly in the same place will produce uneven rope strain, so check regularly for wear.

Figure-Eight Knot.
1. Make a bight, passing the loop behind the static part of the rope.
2. Pass the end over the near side and through the loop.
3. Draw the knot tight.
4. Finish off with a half hitch.

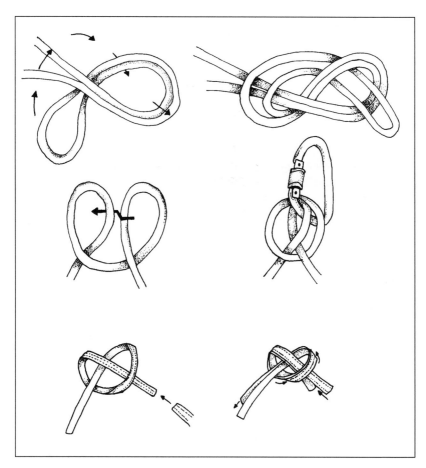

Three of the most commonly used knots are the figure-eight (*top*), the clove hitch (*center*), and the tape knot (*bottom*).

A figure-eight knot can be used as a stopper knot on the end of a rope, for tying two ropes together, or for tying into your climbing harness.

Bowline Knot.

1. Make a loop in the rope.
2. Pass the tail up through the loop.
3. Pass the tail around behind the static rope and back through the loop.
4. Complete the loop by tying a half hitch on the end; this will prevent slipping.

A bowline can also be used to tie your rope to your climbing harness. Avoid a three-way pull on this knot, as that may untie it.

Half Hitch.

1. Loop the loose end all the way around the rope.
2. Draw it back through itself.

The most basic of knots, this is the standard way of finishing off other knots.

Clove Hitch. The clove hitch is not really a knot, but a hitch used to connect anchors at a belay. The beauty is that when it's weighted, it tightens around itself, yet it remains easy to undo.

Remember the most basic principle of all knots: They are weaker than the rope they are tied to.

Horizontal Maneuvers

Tension Traverse. The tension traverse is a horizontal maneuver used to switch crack systems. Let's say you are climbing up a crack that terminates. You put in protection and then notice that 6 feet to the right is another crack system. To reach that, have your belayer lower you about 6 or 8 feet. Then, using rope tension from below, you should be able to scratch and crawl your way across to the new crack. Once there, immediately put in the next protection.

Pendulum. The pendulum is another horizontal move, used when the new crack system is farther away. You first move away from the new crack to gain momentum, then sort of catapult yourself toward the new crack. You may have to run back and forth several times, gaining momentum and increasing the length of the arc until you can reach your goal.

– 6 –

Big Walls

Many climbers who develop aid-climbing skills do so with the intention of applying them to big walls. Numerous big-wall candidates exist in North America, including "The Diamond" on Longs Peak in Colorado, the sandstone spires and towers of Utah, Squamish Chief in British Columbia, lots of choices in Yosemite and Alaska, even some shorter walls in the Cascades of Washington. Unfortunately, there are no big walls east of the Mississippi.

It's going to take more equipment to climb a big wall than it took to climb that first A1 slab. You are now entering the world of pitons, hooks, haul bags, pulleys, portable ledges, and hammocks. The complexities of managing all that equipment can be overcome with good organizational skills.

But those skills will not be immediately evident. Your first big wall will be a learning experience. You can count on making some mistakes, such as tangling ropes, etriers, or haul bags; dropping pitons; running out of food or water; or defecating in the wrong places. You will learn to survive on your first big wall.

I don't recommend starting your big-wall career on any rocky mammoths like El Capitan or Half Dome. In Yosemite, I advise newcomers to start on Sentinel Rock or Washington's Column, ten to fifteen pitches, usually requiring only one bivouac. Do several overnighters before you tackle one of the behemoths.

One way to get off the ground is to volunteer to be a full-time second on someone else's team. Find someone with experience on big walls who is looking for a partner. Veteran climbers will likely lead everything; your job will be to follow and clean pitches. And to learn. Take in everything the veterans do: placements, setting up belays and bivouacs. Serve your apprenticeship well, and soon you will be leading pitches. Some veterans will let you lead a pitch every so often.

Another way of getting acquainted with big walls is to find someone who climbs at about your skill level, and the two of you can thrash your way up a wall, alternating the lead. If you both know enough to do it safely, it's not a bad way to learn. You and your partner improve together, and you both gain the satisfaction that comes from knowing you led half the climb.

I've had scads of apprentices in my climbing career. Of the forty-four partners with whom I've climbed El Capitan, twenty-three had almost no previous big-wall climbing experience. Yet they all made it to the top. Following an experienced climber is a pretty safe way to do a big wall. You're going to learn a lot; you're just not going to lead a lot.

You must be vigilant at all times on a big wall, especially when climbing with a beginner. That bumper sticker "Shit Happens" could have been written by a beginning climber. One time on a big wall, I noticed that my partner, who was new to the sport, kept changing his shoes. He went from tennis shoes to free-climbing boots, and back again. He would put on the more comfortable tennis shoes when it was time to follow me on a pitch with jumars. I told him, "Tad, you keep that up and you're going to drop a shoe." Well, next I hear this cussing and screaming. Sure enough, he dropped a shoe. After the climb, he had to walk out 8 miles in one free-climbing boot and one tennis shoe. Anyone who has hiked in free-climbing boots knows how miserable it is.

I treat every piece of equipment, from rope to Snickers bar, as something that must not be dropped, and I try to instill that in my partners. You especially don't want to lose anything crucial, which includes about everything you have.

Exposure

Standing on a tiny ledge high up on a sheer wall, you have a sense of the earth falling away beneath your feet. This is known in the trade as *exposure*. My opinion is that everyone is at least somewhat intimidated by heights. You might find the occasional oddball who claims that heights don't bother him, but most people playing with a full deck are disturbed by the absence of terra firma on a wall.

The only effective strategy is to keep exposing yourself to exposure. Do it until you get used to it. Exposure bothered me at first, but I kept getting in its face until I became comfortable with it, just as sky divers get used to jumping out of planes. Moreover, my confidence improved as I learned to trust the equipment. And with good reason—today's state-of-the-art climbing gear is worthy of our trust. If you have adequate anchors, there's no reason to believe anything bad is going to happen. On the other hand, it's okay if exposure throws a little fear into you, because overcoming fear with a cool calm can bolster your confidence.

I'm often asked whether I look down. Of course I do; it's one of the great joys of rock climbing. If it bothers you to look down, don't do it. If that feeling persists, consider limiting yourself to shorter climbs. Or perhaps a hobby back in the horizontal world.

It's important to remember that exposure is a gradual process for a big-wall climber. Unlike the sky diver, who suddenly finds himself faced with a 10,000-foot leap of faith, the climber starts at ground zero and moves up inch by inch. Nor is it like the tourist who jets to the top of the Empire State Building by elevator and suddenly steps out on the ninetieth floor. In climbing, you're 10 feet up, then 50 feet up, then 100 feet up. It might take a couple of hours to climb a rope length, a couple more to climb the next rope length. It's so gradual that most people can handle it.

It's true that exposure is more frightening higher up the wall, but realistically your chances of surviving a fall aren't much different whether you're 100 or 1,000 feet up a wall. The 1,000-foot fall will definitely kill you; the 100-foot fall almost certainly will—and if it doesn't, you may wish it had. The idea is not to fall.

Free Time

Big-wall climbing has been called vertical backpacking, a reference to the simple life enjoyed by both backpackers and climbers. Self-contained, we take all necessary provisions with us. We don't worry about the phone bill or being late. Instead, we just move up the rock face, partners working in harmony toward a common goal. It's hard work, but if we have enough provisions, it's also fun. And in the evening, when we've done our pitches and are sitting on a nice, big ledge with a can of beans, shoes and shirt off, light mountain breezes wafting over our skin, we can't help thinking, "It doesn't get any better than this."

Climbers actually have loads of chill time on a big wall. Even if you climb twelve hours a day, that leaves another twelve at your bivouac spot. Some people may climb only eight hours a day, leaving sixteen hours to hang out. How do you fill that time?

I don't recommend it, but some climbers take a stereo for music or a small radio for weather reports—assuming decent reception. Others take portable chess or checkers, crossword puzzles, books, or diaries.

The most important asset you can have on a big wall is a compatible partner. Climbing a rock wall with another person is about as intimate as sharing a space capsule. You and your partner will have a lot of time to talk—or not to talk. My experience is that after a long day of climbing, even quiet people need to chat. Guys invariably talk about past girlfriends, future hopes, what they wanted to do with their lives, and what they really did. It can be a very personal time shared by friends. If you can't get to know someone on a big wall, you probably never will.

Sitting under a canopy of stars, you may be more reflective than usual. Some of my deepest pondering on the meaning of life has been done on rock walls. Questions like "Where have I been?" and "Where do I want to go?" seem to nag me the higher I climb. As a result, climbing has been a real growing experience.

Spending the Night

The first rule of spending the night on a wall is to clip everything to the protection, especially the climbers. Always stay connected to your harness. You can take the leg loops off, but not the swami-belt part. Connect that snugly to several different anchors. Avoid foolish economy, such as trying to rely on only one anchor for two people.

Don't leave your ropes hanging below you, flapping in the breeze, maybe getting wet or freezing. Instead, coil them neatly and keep them from getting tangled.

As you can see, there are lots of chores to be done at the end of the day. You're not finished just because you have reached a ledge. Besides putting the wrap on today, you must prepare for tomorrow.

You may want to organize the next day's equipment the evening before while it's still light.

Never leave anything sitting loose on a ledge, begging to be knocked off in the middle of the night. Shoes can be secured by clipping a carabiner to the laces and attaching that to your equipment bag.

Whether or not it looks like rain, be ready to batten down the hatches. Have your rain fly partially attached and ready to go. You don't want to have to get up in the middle of the night to arrange gear because a storm suddenly blew in. It only takes a minute to get dangerously soaked, putting you at risk for hypothermia, an insidious affliction. Before it is completely dark, make a mental note of where you've stashed the important gear, such as headlamp, extra clothes, and raingear.

It can be dangerous to ignore the possibility of bad weather. I made just that mistake on the South Face of Half Dome in 1986, with John Middendorf and Steve Bosque. We went to bed without our rain flies on, without our raingear available, not even knowing where it was. All of a sudden a storm hit us, and we had to get up in the middle of the night. We shuffled around in the dark, dropping things. It was ugly.

It got uglier still when the temperature dropped and snow started to fall. Before we knew it, we were hopelessly devastated. We had frozen ropes, soaked clothing, and I had hypothermia. We were later rescued, plucked off the rock by a Navy helicopter, like ticks from a dog.

– 7 –

Safety

The great thing about aid climbing is that you use lots of protection—usually a piece every few feet—most of which is bombproof. Even on the most difficult aid pitches, some of your protection will be adequate.

Learn to trust your equipment. As far as I know, so modern nylon rope has ever broken while being properly used. Still, as with any risk sport, safety should be taken seriously. Don't let the pressures of an impatient belayer rush you into making mistakes. When you're on lead, you're in charge.

Loose Rock

Loose rock can be a big problem for aid climbers, because we count on every piece of protection we insert to hold our weight. We are constantly testing the security of protection and the stability of rock with, at the very least, our body weight. In addition, our equipment can bang out loose rock, or the loops of our aid ladders can catch on it and yank it out.

You must first learn to recognize loose rock, most of which is obvious. It can be anything from a solitary boulder sitting on a ledge, to loose stones in a crack, to a partially detached flake that breaks off. You can usually test loose rock by feel. If it's suspect, touch it. Does it wiggle like a loose tooth? If so, it's loose rock. If not, run another test: Hit it with the heel of your hand and see if it vibrates.

Let's say you discover loose rock. What are you going to do about it? The preferred option is to avoid it if you can. Inspect the surroundings for signs of what preceding parties have done. Any piton scars? If someone else has successfully used pitons, you probably can too. But be conservative with your hammer. Tap gently, test with a tug, move gingerly, speak in a soft voice, caress the rock. Take special care not to kick loose stones as you climb past.

Most long climbs have at least one or two sections of loose rock with the potential to kill you. I've been on climbs where the rocks all seem to be piled one on top of another, and everything seems to be moving and creaking. You simply can't be in a hurry around rock like that. If it takes five hours to pass a short section of rock, then that's what it takes. At least you're alive.

I once had a memorable brush with loose rock. I was nailing a piton into what seemed like a flake. I was unaware that there was a hairline fracture at the bottom and that instead of a flake, I had a slab of granite sitting on a sloping ledge. In other words, loose rock. The piton I put into a vertical crack caused the rock to fall apart. Suddenly I was holding a 75-pound piece of stone. The only thing I could do was toss it off to the side. Fortunately, I was on a good piton, the rock was more than 90 degrees, and my partner was not directly below me.

The only time you should eject loose rock is if that's the only way to get around the problem. Suppose you put a piton in a crack and loose rock starts pushing the piton back toward you. Try taking your weight off the protection that's moving, and see if you can shove the pieces back into place. Size up those pieces. Can you handle them? You don't want to tangle with something you can't control. If it's really dangerous—in other words, it could kill you—drill a bolt hole and go around it. I'm quick to do that if it looks as though the loose rock is unmanageable. This is more common on a first ascent, but it could happen anytime. In any event, bolting will solve the problem for you and for future climbers.

Expanding Flakes

Imagine a big slab that is seemingly detached from the wall, like a big Frisbee stuck on the rock. You can't see how it's attached, but it is. Climbing the crack of a feature like this is precarious because it's liable to move. There's also a risk that you might pull the whole thing off, but many expanding flakes are giant and can't be pulled off. The more common risk is as follows: You're in your etriers in an expanding flake, putting weight on a piton. You reach up higher in this flake and put in another piton. As you pound in the second piton, the flake begins to expand. You're actually making the crack bigger. That causes the piton you're on to loosen, maybe even to fall out. That's why you should attack expanding flakes with camming devices or wedges. Put a camming device in an expanding flake, weight it, then put in another one. The second one may cause the flake to expand, but that first one just grips harder, compensating nicely for the growth of the crack.

Whatever protection you use, be gentle. It's sometimes inevitable that you expand a flake. Before chocks or SLCDs, we had no choice but to use pitons. I recommend the following technique when relying on pitons in an expanding flake: Suppose you're weighting piton number one in an expanding flake and have to drive in a second piton above it. As you're driving in number two, you should already have your etriers and a carabiner attached to it. Run it down to your climbing harness so that if the piton you're on pops, the top one can catch you. As you're hammering in that top one, just as it appears to be good, quickly, gently shift your weight from the lower piton to the higher one. It is admittedly an uncomfortable feeling.

Bad Landings

Say you bivouacked on a ledge—a nice, big, hard ledge. Next day, as you start to leave that ledge, it ceases to be your ally. If you're climbing a rotten crack and your placements are questionable, you run the risk of landing back on that ledge. Short of carrying a mattress, you can do little about this except to take great care in placing and testing protection. Make sure every placement is the best it can be.

Belaying

It's crucial that the belayer, in whose hands the life of the leader hangs, be on the alert the whole time the leader is climbing. He must secure himself so that if the leader falls, the belayer is not yanked from his perch. By using a good belay device, a belayer can stop a fall with minimal effort just by holding on to the belay rope after it has passed through the device.

It's important that the belayer and leader stay in communication.

The belayer should be informed immediately of any trouble the leader is having. Although the belayer should keep his hands on the rope even if things seem to be going perfectly, it's helpful to know when heightened awareness is required. Such communication may prevent the belayer from being slammed against the rocks or, worse, pulled from his perch.

Belaying takes a lot of patience. The belayer should not be making a peanut butter and jelly sandwich with one hand, belaying with the other, while the leader is doing a series of hook moves on A5. Belayers should wait until the appropriate time to tend to their personal needs. The job demands putting the welfare of the leader above all else. After all, the leader is counting on you to be in control of his lifeline.

It's a good idea for belayers to wear gloves. One time I was belaying without gloves on Half Dome, when my leader—a big man—fell. There was no protection between us. I had a precarious body belay going, no directionals in the rock. As he fell, I lost the rope and was yanked backward. I eventually regained control of the rope, twisted it, and made it stop. But when I looked down, I saw that it had shredded my hands like old rags.

The leader fell 75 feet, but I was hurt worse than he was. My hands were a poor grade of hamburger, and I had no first-aid kit, but I still had to jumar and clean the next ten pitches.

Testing Protection

The main purpose of testing protection is, of course, to prevent a bad fall. Let's say you put in a piton and like it. It's solid. Now you reach up and put in a second piton. But this one doesn't go in very well. You put it in as best you can and attach your aiders to it. To test its strength, you want to be down below it, positioned so that if you put weight on this newest protection and it pulls out, you won't shockload the previous one. You attach your aiders to the questionable protection, put one foot in, and give it a little bounce. When you bounce, you are putting all your weight on it—plus a little more. If the protection fails, you know that it is no good; on the other hand, if it holds a bounce, it is reasonable to assume that it will hold your body weight.

It can be dicey deciding the safety of using the bolts, rivets, and dowels left behind by previous climbers. Bolts, made of steel, are used in holes 1 to 1½ inches deep. I hear stories of climbers breaking bolts, but it has never happened to me. Sometimes at belay stations, I will reject old bolts as too dangerous.

Rivets and dowels, on the other hand, are made of aluminum, intended for holes ³/₈ to ½ inch deep, and used only for holding body weight. I did Harding's route on the "Wall of the Early Morning Light" eight years after he did, and I used a lot of his rivets. They seemed old then. Now, twenty-five years after Harding, people are still using those rivets. It's a judgment call.

Sharp Edges

They're out there—rock projections and protrusions feasting on tasty rope fibers. Just make sure they're not *your* rope fibers. Avoidance is the first option to consider when confronted with a sharp edge. By clever use of runners, you can often dodge the trouble spot. Another option is cushioning the rope with a shirt or belay seat stuffed in between rope and edge. If neither option is feasible, you can perform the ethically dubious task of pounding off the sharp edges with your hammer.

Retreat and Rescue

Retreat is the abandonment of a climb, normally accomplished by rappeling. There are at least as many reasons to retreat as there are to climb. Injury, illness, personality clashes. Joe and Bill have been climbing for two days when they suddenly realize they can't stand each other. Or maybe Joe breaks a finger. Or they decide they don't have enough water to finish. Or they just don't feel like being up there.

I could write a book on 1,001 reasons to retreat. How about dropping your hammer? That's a good reason. I once saw a team lose its haul bag. It became disconnected from its anchor and dropped like a rock, leaving them without any visible means of support.

Retreat is nothing to be ashamed of. Sometimes it is exactly the right thing to do. I've made fifty ascents of El Capitan, but I've also bailed out early six times. The number one reason has been heat. Another time, 2,000 feet up the Muir Wall, I couldn't find the route. (I later went back and found it.) And after my 40-foot fall, I decided that the rock wasn't the best place to be.

As for rescue, every climber has a different breaking point—when he's had enough. The two most common reasons for rescue are injury and bad weather (which can lead to hypothermia in winter and dehydration in summer). Yelling for help is often enough to alert authorities. Rescue teams are ubiquitous in rugged terrain.

Probably the most famous rescue was one that didn't happen: Warren Harding and Dean Caldwell on El Capitan's "Wall of the Early Morning Light" in 1970. They were two-thirds of the way up the cliff when a storm hit. They had survived the storm on a ledge when they noticed climbers being lowered over the top. Although Harding and Caldwell had not requested help, the park service had assumed they must be in trouble and sent it anyway.

Harding yelled up to the climbers that not only had they not requested help but that they would refuse rescue, and would they please just get the hell out of there.

The rescuers retreated, and Harding and Caldwell finished their climb—after twenty-seven days.

A controversy continues over who pays for rescues. In most national parks, the taxpayers do. Climbers can be cited and taken to court for negligence, though they seldom are. You would be guilty of negligence and could be fined if, for example, you tried to climb a cliff in winter without a rain suit, got drenched, became hypothermic, and had to be rescued. In Denali (McKinley) National Park in Alaska, climbers are required to post a bond in case of rescue. This seems to be the direction we're heading.

– 8 –

Etiquette and Ethics

The vertical world is an increasingly social one. Even when hanging from a high-altitude granite face, we must bear in mind how our behavior will affect other people. This raises significant issues of etiquette and ethics.

Etiquette

Passing Other Climbers. Suppose you want to pass a slower party on your route. Or perhaps you're the slower party, and other climbers are closing from below. You're bound to encounter both situations if you climb long enough, especially if you favor classic routes in popular areas.

If you are the faster team, your best bet is to explain politely to the slower team that it has taken you one day to go as far as they went in two. Point out that they will never have to deal with you again if only they will let you pass. Such an arrangement is clearly in everyone's best interest, for after the pass is completed, both teams can move at their own pace, with less pressure.

The problem is that the slower team has to shut down their climb for up to two hours. You can suggest that they take a lunch break, or offer to compensate by anchoring one of their ropes at the high point of the pitch on which you will pass them. That way, they lose no time; in fact, they may gain.

It's best if you can pass at a ledge, but that's not always possible. A pass with no ledge is somewhat riskier. If possible, stop just be-

71

low the slower team and set up alternate belays so that you don't have to use their anchors or climb right over them.

A team once refused to let my team pass. The leader was vehement. He knew very well that we were faster, but he said that every time he'd tried to do this climb, he'd been deterred by other, slower climbers. He was also afraid that if we passed, we'd knock loose rocks down on him. Although we never saw any loose rock, he remained determined not to let us pass.

I should have realized it wasn't our time and abandoned the climb. But we'd hiked a long way and decided to stay with it. The other climbers were rank beginners with poor techniques. So we spent two days following them up a climb that should have taken us one day. In all, we spent about half our time waiting. Everyone finished, but we were forced to spend an extra night on the rock. I'd like to go back and do that climb in eight or ten hours so that I could feel good about it.

I've also been caught in the slow lane by someone wanting to pass my team. If I see a rapidly approaching party, I try to anticipate their request. I yell down to them, "Hey, it's obvious you're going faster. We're going to hang here while you go by." It just makes sense to me, and they appreciate it. Plus it gives me an opportunity to ask them, "When you get to the top, would you leave any leftover water?"

However you handle the interpersonal details of passing other climbers, be unfailingly polite. If you try to bully your way past people, they may let you pass, but you detract from the sport.

Waste Disposal. Urination and defecation are unavoidable facts of life; on a slab or wall, they take on even greater importance.

Urinating has its own law: Do not pee in cracks or on ledges where other climbers climb, sleep, and belay.

But the crux of the matter is how to defecate in a vertical world. As a trail backpacker, you must think about this matter a bit more than at home. You have to walk from camp, find your spot, bury the deed, and dispose of the toilet paper. For climbers, however, burial is not an option.

It used to be that climbers relied solely on the gravity method. A quick check below for other people, and then bombs away. Then for a time, we dumped our loads in paper bags and tossed them below after making sure we weren't giving some innocent a brown crown. Afterward, we returned to the base of the climb to retrieve our discarded bags.

If there are dozens of climbers on a rock, however, irresponsible elimination habits mean smelly, unsightly conditions, even health risks. So a new method has evolved that, for now, is voluntary. Climbers are carrying tubes made out of PVC pipe, with a permanent cap on one end, a removable cap on the other. The idea is to dump your waste in a paper bag, roll up the bag, and put it in the tube. Add a little kitty litter to absorb the odor, then carry the tube with you, disposing of it properly at the end of the climb. This method will be law, at least in Yosemite, by May 1995.

Whatever method you use, don't forget to properly dispose of toilet paper. It can be a real hassle. I have seen climbers fling dirty paper off a wall, only to have updrafts carry it toward colleagues above them. What could be more disgusting than swatting away contaminated toilet paper displaying the persistence of a used-car salesman?

As with all issues of ethics and etiquette, proper waste disposal just takes effort. Rude, unethical behavior is usually nothing more than laziness.

Ethics

Cast a critical eye around popular climbing sites, and you are bound to see the environmental damage wrought, in part, by rock jocks. Unauthorized trails weave up mountainsides, scratched out by climbers with eyes only for the next pitch. Nylon slings used as rappel anchors hang from cliffs like party streamers. And bolts, often set with portable power drills, dot the rock like a bad case of acne.

Environmental degradation has become so serious that the National Park Service, the Forest Service, the Bureau of Land Management (BLM), and the U.S. Fish and Wildlife Service are considering a clampdown on climbers.

First let's look at some of the main ethical issues that climbers face.

Pitons. Pitons, which scar the rock, are indeed controversial. But many slabs, and just about every big wall, has spots that demand pitons. It's a common fallacy that pitons are widely banned. The fact is, manufacturers still make them, and plenty of climbers own and use them.

When should you use them? When it's the best protection you have. Confronted with a crack too shallow for a camming device or a stopper, the choice may be pitons or retreat. Pitons will damage the rock slightly, but preservation of self must take precedence over preservation of rock. It would be foolish to take a long fall because you felt guilty about nailing a piton.

Some climbers are inevitably better than others at avoiding the use of pitons. You may use a piton where someone else uses a marginal chock placement. It's ultimately a personal decision. If, however, a route has been climbed without using pitons, it would behoove you to climb in the same manner. If you don't feel comfortable climbing such a route without pitons, pick a route where it's appropriate to use them.

The older, well-established routes with their big cracks are generally more receptive to piton alternatives. Newer climbs tend to feature thin cracks that require knife-blade and Lost Arrow pitons.

Bolting. Bolts, which are designed to be left in the rock, are at the heart of the environmental debate. The first ascent team on a climb determines how many bolts will be used and where they will go. On occasion, subsequent parties have removed bolts put up by previous parties. Such an act is a strong statement that the first team went too far. Ironically, however, the removal of bolts causes greater damage to the rock than their placement.

The most famous case of bolt removal occurred after Warren Harding climbed El Capitan's "Wall of the Early Morning Light" in 1970. He scaled a fairly blank section of rock by drilling 330 bolt holes. A few months later, Royal Robbins, a rival of Harding's, decided that the route was invalid and that he would erase the climb by removing the bolts. After removing about 300 feet of bolts, Robbins changed his mind and decided to leave the rest in place (he even went on to use some of Harding's bolts). Still, his act created a huge controversy. Robbins, who found the route to be of high standard, later admitted that it hadn't been wisest thing to do.

A subsequent party usually adds bolts only if something has physically changed on that climb. If, for example, a flake breaks off or a placement is ruined by the repeated use of pitons, it might be necessary to add a bolt. Or maybe some old rusty bolts need replacing. Faced with a section of blank rock, climbers might feel the need to add a bolt from which to belay or sleep. Adding bolts you believe are necessary does not make you a bad person or a bad climber. I estimate that there are about five thousand bolts on El Capitan, of which I have drilled about a hundred—all on my first three ascents.

Leaving Equipment Behind. Bolts, rivets, and dowels are the only items designed to be left behind. But it's an imperfect world, and sometimes other hardware—commonly pitons—jam in the rock.

If you give up after trying your best to extract a defiant piece of gear, don't berate yourself. It happens all the time. Maybe after a good freeze and thaw, the piece will loosen for a future party.

Governmental Restrictions. The most likely governmental restrictions against climbers include limiting or banning bolts. Says Karl Gawell, director of national parks programs for the Wilderness Society, "It's difficult for us to understand when drilling a hole in the rock is not defacing a resource."

Critics of bolts like to point to a section of the 1964 Wilderness Act that prohibits leaving "permanent improvements" in wilderness areas. The Forest Service may yet interpret this as meaning that bolts should be banned in its 34.6 million acres. If the Forest Service issues such a ban, the BLM and Fish and Wildlife Service could follow. Only the Park Service seems inclined to recognize climbing as a legitimate recreational activity.

Climbers, not surprisingly, feel that they are being unfairly targeted. When you consider the roads, tunnels, hotels, gift shops, and restaurants that the Park Service allows, why pick on a few little bolts?

Anyway, the real villain is the portable power drill, which enables someone to set a bolt in seconds instead of nearly an hour. That has led to an epidemic of climbers creating new routes by rap bolting (rappeling down a route, cleaning cracks and holds with a wire brush, and setting bolts with a drill).

The idea of any restrictions is, of course, abhorrent to climbers, many of whom were originally attracted to the sport for its heady freedom. Clearly, then, we climbers, driven by both altruism and self-interest, had better start managing our own house. Most climbers concede that power drills and proliferating rap bolting is environmentally harmful (and often illegal), so why not clamp down on power drills? A blanket ban on bolts and fixed anchors will only make our sport more hazardous. "In some places a ban on bolting is a ban on climbing entirely," says Charley Shimanski, executive director of the American Alpine Club.

This should be a wake-up call for climbers and friends of climbing. The raging popularity of the sport could be its very downfall. It certainly will be if leads to a curbing of the freedom that was one of its main draws. We can prevent that by remembering that we are citizens of both the vertical and the horizontal worlds.

Glossary

abseil: see *rappel*.

accessory cord: thin rope, from 3 to 8 millimeters, often used for making slings, or runners.

active rope: the length of rope between a moving climber and the belayer.

aid climbing: the technique of moving up a rock face resting on artificial holds. Slings, ropes, nuts, and other paraphernalia are used for physical support, not just for emergency protection or belay anchors. (Contrasted with *free climbing.)*

alternate leads: a method of climbing rock or ice in which two climbers lead alternate pitches of a climb.

anchor: the point at which a fixed rope, a rappel rope, or a belay is secured to rock, snow, or ice by any of various means.

angle piton: a metal wedge that is V- or U-shaped in cross section. Designed to fit in cracks from ½ inch wide (baby angles) to 4 inches wide (bongs). Angles are very stable because they contact the rock in three places.

approach: the distance a climber must hike from the car to the start of the climb. An approach may take anywhere from a few minutes to several days.

ascender: a mechanical device, such as a Jumar, Gibbs, or Shunt, that works on a ratchet principle. The device will slide up a rope but will grip securely when it gets a downward pull, thus permitting climbers to move up a rope and not slide down. Ascender knots (see *prusik)* serve the same purpose.

bandolier: a chest loop for carrying climbing equipment.

bashie: a soft, malleable aluminum blob that is hammered into a crack too shallow to take a piton. Bashies come in various sizes. Also called a *mashie*.

bat hook: a device used for direct aid, invented by Warren Harding for use in shallow drilled holes on blank rock where bolts would otherwise be necessary.

belay: to tend the climbing rope, ready to immediately put enough friction on the rope to hold the climber in case of a fall. Friction is generated by the rope passing around the belayer's body or through a belay device. Belaying is the primary safeguard in climbing, and its practice is universal. *Belay* also refers to the entire system set up to make belaying possible, including the anchor that holds the belayer in place.

belay device: any of numerous small metal gadgets that force a bend in the climbing rope, creating enough friction to enable a belayer to hold a fall. See also *descender* and *figure-eight*.

bight: a loop of rope.

big wall: a steep cliff or face, vertical or nearly so, that is 1,000 feet or more from bottom to top.

biner (pronounced "beaner"): slang for *carabiner*.

bivouac: a night out without a tent.

bivouac sack: a lightweight, unfilled, waterproof nylon bag that can cover a sleeping bag, or a climber caught without a sleeping bag. Also called *bivy sack*.

bivy: slang for *bivouac*.

body belay: see *waist belay*.

bolt: a thin metal rod that is hammered into a predrilled hole in the rock to serve as a multidirectional anchor. Bolts, ranging in size from ¼- to ½-inch, were originally used to protect free climbers on otherwise unprotectable routes and to piece together crack systems on longer climbs. Because they are left in place for subsequent climbers to use, bolts remain controversial.

bolted route: a route that is entirely protected by bolts.

bolt hanger: a metal piece that is attached to the bolt, allowing a carabiner to be clipped to the bolt.

bombproof: said of a hold or belay that will not fail, regardless of how much weight or force is put on it.

bong: the biggest piton, designed for cracks wider than a person's foot. Also called *bong-bong*.

brake bar: a small aluminum rod that is used to create friction on the rope when a climber is descending by rappel.

bucket: a large bombproof hold.

bulge: a small overhang.

bumblies: beginners, usually unsupervised, who have no idea what they are doing.

buttress: a section of a mountain or cliff standing out from the rest, often flanked on both sides by gullies or couloirs; somewhat wider than an arête.

carabiner: an oval or D-shaped metal snap-link about 3 inches long in the shape of a giant safety pin. Capable of holding a ton or more, carabiners are used for attaching the rope to anchors in rock or snow.

carabiner brake: a configuration of four to six carabiners arranged to provide rope friction for rappeling.

chest harness: a harness used in conjunction with a waist harness to attach a climber to the rope.

chickenhead: protruding knob on a rock face that can be used for a hold.

chock: a rock wedged in a crack or behind a flake, around which a runner can be threaded and then clipped to a rope for an anchor point. Before artificial chocks, British climbers used to carry pebbles to place in cracks; later they used hexagonal machine nuts found on railroad tracks. Today there are two basic types of chocks: wedges and hexes. Also called a *chockstone*.

chockcraft: the art of using chocks to create secure anchors in the rock.

chock sling: wire, rope, or webbing that attaches to a chock.

chop: to remove from the rock someone else's protection, such as bolts.

classic routes: ways up mountains that have special character, historical interest, great difficulty, popularity, or a combination of these.

clean climbing: means of ascension that leaves the rock unscarred and undamaged after the climbing team has passed.

cleaning the pitch: removing all the protection hardware placed by the leader.

cliff: a smooth, steep face of rock.

cliffhanger: see *sky hook*.

clip in: to attach oneself to the mountain by means of a carabiner snapped onto an anchor.

clove hitch: one of the two main knots (the other is the figure-eight) used in the ropework system.

coiling: the various methods of looping and tying a rope so that it can be carried, all requiring a certain amount of skill to avoid kinking.

copperhead: a malleable piece of metal used as aid; like a mashie, but for use in even smaller pockets and shallow seams.

corner: an outside junction of two planes of rock, approximately at right angles. (Contrasted with *dihedral*.)

crab: slang for *snap-link carabiner*.

crack: a gap or fracture in the rock, varying in width from a thin seam to a wide chimney.

crag: a low cliff, one or two pitches high.

crux: the most difficult part of a pitch or climb (though some climbs have more than one crux).

dehydration: a depletion of body fluids that can hinder the body's ability to regulate its own temperature. One can become dehydrated during climbing if the fluids lost from perspiration and respiration are not replaced by drinking water. Chronic dehydration lowers a climber's tolerance to fatigue, reduces his ability to sweat, elevates his rectal temperature, and increases the stress on his circulatory system. In general, a loss of 2 percent or more of one's body weight by sweating affects performance; a loss of 5 to 6 percent affects health.

descender: a friction device used for descending ropes (rappeling). The most common is the figure-eight; others include the brake bar and the carabiner brake. Also known as a *rappel device*.

dihedral: a high-angled inside corner where two rock planes intersect; shaped like an open book. (Contrasted with *corner*).

direct: the most direct way up a route or climb, usually the way water would take to fall down the rock. The direct tends to be steeper and more difficult than ordinary routes.

direct aid: the aid or equipment a climber puts weight on to progress up a rock.

double up: to anchor two chocks close together for added protection.

down and out: the correct position of a carabiner gate when it is connected to an anchor.

Dulfursitz rappel: method of descending in which a climber threads an anchored climbing rope between his legs, returns it to the front of his body, then wraps it over a shoulder and holds it behind him with one hand.

escarpment: an inland cliff formed by the erosion of the inclined strata of hard rocks.

etrier: a short, foldable ladder of three to five steps with a small loop at the top for attaching to an aid point. It is usually made from webbing sewn or knotted to form loops for the feet. Most aid climbers will carry two or four etriers. A climber who has moved up to the top of an etrier will place another aid point, to which the next etrier will be clipped.

expansion bolt: a bolt that expands and locks when screwed into a prebored hole in the rock. Used when a rock lacks cracks into which a piton or nut can be inserted. Bolts provide the safest protection, but they alter the rock and change the character and degree of difficulty of a climb.

exposed: said of a climber's route that is steep and hard with a big drop below it.

exposure: a long drop beneath a climber's feet; what one confronts to the max when climbing a sheer face like El Capitan.

extractor: a tool climbers use to remove chocks that have become stuck in cracks. Also called a *chock pick*.

face: a wall of rock steeper than 60 degrees.

fall factor: a numerical value indicating the severity of a fall. If protection holds, the most serious fall has a value of 2, and most climbing falls are between .5 and 1. Calculate the fall factor by dividing the distance of the fall by the length of rope between you and your belayer.

fifi hook: a small hook designed to hold a climber's body weight on a placement while he puts in the next placement.

figure-eight descender: a metal rappeling device in the shape of the numeral 8. One hole is used to attach the device to a harness with a carabiner; a rope is passed through the other hole to provide friction for the descent.

figure-eight knot: one of the two main knots (the other is the clove hitch) used in the ropework system.

first ascent: the first time a route has been climbed.

fixed protection: anchors, such as bolts or pitons, that are permanently placed in the rock.

fixed rope: a rope that a climber has anchored and left in place after a pitch is climbed so that climbers can ascend and descend at will. Most expedition climbing uses fixed ropes to facilitate load carrying and fast retreat over dangerous terrain.

flake: a thin, partly detached leaf of rock. Also means to prepare a rope so that it won't tangle when you are using it.

flapper: torn skin on the hand—the kind that flaps.

flaring crack: a crack with sides that flare out.

free climbing: climbing in which natural handholds and footholds are used. Hardware is used only for protection and not for support or progress. (Contrasted with *aid climbing*.)

friction brake: a device that provides rope friction when rappeling, such as a bar mounted on one or more carabiners.

Friend: an active (spring-loaded) camming device inserted into a crack as an anchor point. Designed and marketed by Ray Jardine in 1978, the Friend was a major breakthrough because it allowed climbers to protect roofs and parallel cracks with minimal time spent making the placement.

frost wedging: the opening and widening of a crack by the repeated freezing and thawing of ice in the crack.

gardening: cleaning a climb of vegetation and loose rocks.

gear freak: a climber who has lots of equipment but not much knowledge.

glacis: an easy-angled slab of rock between horizontal and 30 degrees. A slab is steeper, and a wall steeper yet.

Gore-Tex: a material used for clothing and tents that allows water vapor from the body to escape but will not allow liquid water droplets (rain) to enter. It has high breathability.

gorp: a high-carbohydrate snack food made primarily from nuts and dried fruit; an acronym for "good ol' raisins and peanuts."

groove: a shallow, vertical crack.

gully: steep-sided rift or chasm, deep and wide enough to walk inside.

hanging belay: a belay station on vertical rock that offers no ledge for support.

harness: a contraption worn around the shoulders or waist, usually made of wide tape, and offering convenient loops through which to clip a climber's rope and gear. If a climber falls while roped onto a harness, the shock load is distributed over a wide area. The climber also has a better chance of remaining in an upright position, lowering the risk of head meeting rock.

haul bag: a bag used for holding and hauling gear up a wall.

hawser-laid rope: rope made from three groups of filaments plaited together.

headlamp: a light that is mounted on a climber's helmet or headband.

headwall: the sheerest, often most difficult, section of a cliff or mountain, usually its uppermost.

hero loop: see *tie-off loop*.

hip belay: see *waist belay*.

hold: a protrusion or indentation in the rock that a climber can grasp with fingers (handhold) or stand on (foothold).

horn: a protruding piece of rock over which a sling can be hung for an anchor.

ice piton: a piton designed to be hammered into ice.

ice screw: a threaded metal device with a pointed tip that is pounded, then screwed, into hard ice. It serves the same purpose as a piton in rock.

impact force: the tug a falling climber feels from the rope as it stops a fall.

inactive rope: rope between any two climbers who are not moving.

jug: a large, indented hold; a type of bucket. Also, slang for the verb to *jumar*.

Jumar: a trade name for a Swiss rope-gripping ascender. This device is so widely used for self-belay and for hauling on expeditions that the word is also used as a verb: "I jumared up to the ledge."

kernmantle: standard climbing rope in which a core (kern), constructed of one or more braided units, is protected by an outer braided sheath (mantle).

knife blade: a long, thin piton.

lead, or leader: the first climber in a party of roped climbers; the head of an expedition.

leader fall: a fall taken by the lead climber. The leader will fall double whatever the distance is to the closest protection.

leading through: said of a second climber continuing to climb through a stance, thereby becoming the leader. If both climbers are of more or less equal competence, this is an efficient way to climb.

ledge: a level area on a cliff or mountain: may be grass, rock, or snow.

load capacity: the maximum load that a piece of gear can withstand.

mashie: see *bashie*.

multidirectional anchor: an anchor that is secure no matter which direction a load comes from. Bolts, some fixed pitons, and some chock configurations are multidirectional anchors.

multipitch route: a climb consisting of more than one pitch.

nailing: hammering a chain of pitons into a crack.

natural anchor: a tree, boulder, or other natural feature that is well placed and strong enough to make a good anchor.

natural line: a rock climb that follows an obvious feature up the face of a cliff, such as a groove, a gully, or a series of cracks.

nose: a jutting protrusion of rock, broad and sometimes with an undercut base.

nut: an artificial chockstone, usually made of aluminum alloy and threaded with nylon cord. Nuts are fitted into cracks in the rock and usually can be used in place of pitons, which can scar the rock. A climber using only nuts needs no hammer, since nuts can be lifted out of their placements.

objective dangers: mountain hazards that are not necessarily the result of flaws in a climber's technique. They include avalanches, rockfall, and crevasses.

opposing chock: a chock that is anchored in the opposite direction from another chock. In combination, the two chocks protect against a multidirectional load.

overdriven: said of a piton when its effectiveness is reduced by too much hammering.

overhang: rock that exceeds 90 degrees.

PDH: acronym for "pretty darn hard"; extreme aid climbing.

pedestal: a flat-topped, detached pinnacle.

peg: see *piton* (this is the British term).

pendulum: a sideways movement across a rock face by swinging on a rope suspended from above.

Perlon: German trade name for a plastic similar to nylon.

pin: see *piton*.

pinnacle: a partially detached feature, like a church steeple.

pitch: a section of climbing between two stances or belay points. A climbing distance that is usually the length of a 150- or 165-foot rope, it is the farthest the leader will go before allowing the second on the rope to catch up.

piton: a metal wedge hammered into a crack until it is secure, used as an anchor point for protection or aid. In the United States, pitons are used only when absolutely necessary, because repeated use damages rock. The first hard-steel pitons were made by John Salathé for use on the Southwest Face of Half Dome in 1946. Also known as *pin* or *peg*.

piton hammer: a hammer designed and carried for pounding in and extracting pitons.

piton scar: a groove in the rock caused by the placement and removal of a piton.

pocket: a shallow hole—and thus hold—in the rock.

pooling: a method of rope management in which the climber places one end of the rope on the ground and piles concentric loops of rope on top.

Portaledge: a cotlike sleeping platform, suspended on a vertical rock face from pitons.

protection: the anchors—such as chocks, bolts, or pitons—to which a climber connects the rope while ascending.

protection system: the configuration of anchors, runners, carabiners, ropes, harnesses, and belayer that combine to stop a falling climber.

prow: a rock feature resembling the prow of a ship, such as the Nose of El Capitan.

prusik: a technique for climbing a rope, originally by use of a prusik knot, now also by means of mechanical ascenders. The knot, invented by Karl Prusik, uses a loop of thin rope wound around a larger-diameter rope in such a way that the knot will slide freely when unweighted but will grip tightly to the main rope when a climber's weight is applied to it.

put up: to make the first ascent of a route.

rack: the collection of climbing gear carried by the lead climber, as arranged on a gear sling. Also, to arrange the gear on the sling.

rappel: to descend by sliding down a rope. Friction for controlling the descent is provided by wraps of rope around the body or by a mechanical rappel device. The rope is usually doubled so that it can be pulled down afterward. Also called *abseil*.

rappel device: see *descender*.

rappel point: the anchor for a rappel—that is, what the rope, or the sling holding it, is fastened to at the top.

rating system: a system of terms or numbers describing the difficulty of climbs. There are seven major rating systems, including the American (Yosemite) Decimal, British, French, East German, and Australian systems.

rat tail: an excessively worn, unsafe climbing rope.

roof: an overhanging section of rock that is close to horizontal. Roofs vary in size from an eave of a few centimeters to giant cantilevers several yards wide.

rope: important element of the belay system. Modern climbing rope is 150 or 165 feet of nylon kernmantle. Lead ropes range from 10 to 12 millimeters in diameter, backup ropes 8 to 9 millimeters. According to John Forrest Gregory in *Rock Sport*, the ideal climbing rope would have all the following qualities: low impact force, low elongation under both impact force and low load, good handling qualities, light weight, water resistance, high ratings for holding falls, resistance to cutting and abrasion, and a low price.

roped solo climbing: free climbing or aid climbing a route alone but protected by a rope. This is an advanced technique, requiring a lot of gear.

roping up: the act of a party of climbers tying themselves together with climbing ropes.

route: a particular way up a cliff. A cliff may have dozens of routes, each with a name and a rating.

runner: a short length of nylon webbing or accessory cord tied or stitched to form a loop; used for connecting anchors to the rope and for other climbing applications. Also called a *sling*.

runout: a section of a climb that is unprotectable, other than with bolts (which may be discouraged).

rurp: an acronym for realized ultimate reality piton, the smallest piton in the arsenal. A rurp, about the size of a postage stamp, fits into a fingernail-thick crack.

safety margin : the amount of extra strength built into climbing gear. For example, a carabiner may have a strength rating of 6,000 pounds, but it rarely has to support more than 3,000 pounds. Thus it has a cushion, or safety margin, of 3,000 pounds.

scramble: an easy climb, usually without a rope. (Contrasted with *technical climbing*.)

scree: a long slope of loose stones on a mountainside.

screwgate: a carabiner that can be "locked" with a barrel on a screw thread. Less common than snap-links, screwgates are used when there is a risk of the gate opening. Also called a *locking carabiner*.

seam: a crack far too thin for fingers but big enough to accept some small chocks, pitons, or copperheads.

seam hook: a small hook shaped like an anchor that can be set in thin cracks. Some seam hooks can be tapped into cracks with a hammer.

second: the climber who follows the lead. Though the lead might take a substantial fall, the second usually risks only a short fall, as the belay is from above. The second usually cleans the pitch.

self-belay: the technique of protecting oneself during a roped solo climb, often with a self-belay device.

sit bag: a cloth seat that climbers

attach to the rock and sit in to make hanging from a wall more comfortable.

sky hook: a tiny hook with a thin curved end that attaches to nubbins or flakes, used when nothing else is available except maybe a bolt. It is precarious because only the climber's body weight keeps it in place.

slab: large, smooth rock face inclined between 30 and 60 degrees.

sling: see *runner*.

smashie: see *bashie*.

snap-link: a carabiner with a spring-loaded gate that opens inward. (Contrasted with *screw-gate carabiner*.)

soloing: climbing alone, whether roped or unroped, aided or free.

spike: a finger of rock.

sport rappeling: descending a rope in a fast, bouncy manner, with speed as the main goal.

stance: the position a climber is in at any given time, especially the position of the belayer.

stirrups: direct-aid slings made into the shape of little rope ladders with aluminum steps. No longer used much in the United States.

stopper: a wedge-shaped nut.

swami belt: part of the harness; 10 to 12 feet of 1- or 2-inch webbing wrapped around the waist in such a way that allows a climber to tie on to it with a rope.

taking in: removing slack in the active rope from a moving climber.

talus: the weathered rock fragments that accumulate at the base of a slope.

technical climbing: climbing that requires hardware, harnesses, ropes, and specialized climbing boots. (Contrasted with a *scramble*.)

tension traverse: direct-aid climbing in which a climber crosses a traverse with the aid of a tight rope from the side, using hands and feet on the rock to counterbalance the side pull of the rope.

tie-off loop: a short loop of nylon webbing tied to a piton near the rock to reduce leverage.

tincture of benzoin: a solution of water, alcohol, and benzoin (resin from a tree in Java) that climbers can apply to their hands to provide a protective coating against rock abrasion.

top rope: a rope anchored above a climber, providing maximum security; sometimes called *TR*. To top-rope means to rig a climb with a top rope or to climb a pitch using a top rope.

trashie: a bashie, strung with a nylon sling, that has been left on a route. The sling soon rots, and the metal blob turns ugly and useless.

traverse: to proceed around rather than straight over an obstacle; to climb from side to side. A traverse may be an easy walk along a ledge or a daunting passage. Protecting traverses is often difficult, because a fall will cause the climber to pendulum, ending up off route even if no injuries occur.

tunnel vision: seeing only a small area directly in front. This is a common pitfall for the beginning climber, who, because of nervousness, may miss an obvious hold that is nearby but off to one side.

Tyrolean traverse: a rope bridge connecting two points (with a backup second rope linked to the climber who is crossing).

unidirectional anchor: an anchor that will hold securely if loaded from one direction but will pull free if loaded from any other direction.

waist belay: a method of taking in and paying out a belayed active rope. The belayer passes the rope around his waist; the hand on the active rope side is the directing hand, and the hand on the slack rope side is the braking hand. Also called the *hip belay* or *body belay*.

wall: a steep cliff or face, between 60 and 90 degrees.

windchill: the cooling of the body that results from wind passing over its surface—especially dramatic if the surface is wet. It is a more useful measurement of meteorological discomfort than is temperature alone.

zipper: a series of poor aid placements, all of which can be expected to pop out, one after the other, if the leader takes a fall.